THE ART OF CLASSICAL DETAILS II
An Ideal Collaboration

THE ART OF CLASSICAL DETAILS II
AN IDEAL COLLABORATION

Phillip James Dodd

Foreword by Ellie Cullman

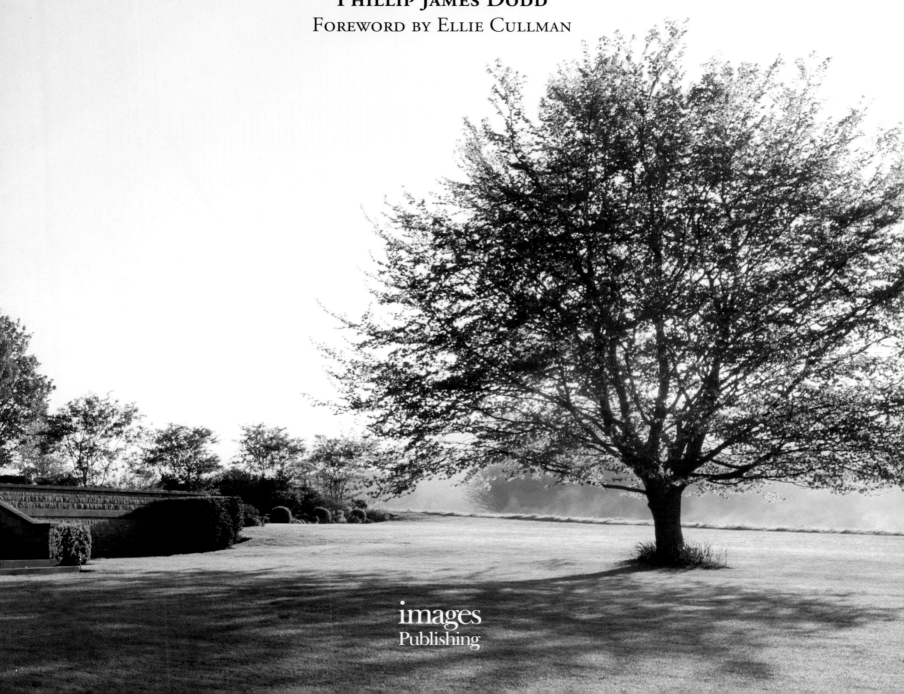

images
Publishing

Dedicated, as always, to my family.

FRONT COVER:
A CLASSICAL TOWNHOUSE (see page 179): The walls of the library in this Chicago Townhouse are finished in a custom peacock-blue lacquer.
S. R. Gambrell with Liederbach & Graham Architects

INSIDE SLEEVE:
A view from the living room into the den of a newly renovated Manhattan pied-a-terre.
Designed by Phillip James Dodd under the auspices of Wadia Associates

HALF TITLE:
A FEDERAL-STYLE RESIDENCE (see page 161): A custom crafted plaster ceiling medallion.
Allan Greenberg Architect

TITLE PAGE:
KINGSHAM FARM (see page 227): The rear façade and garden terrace open onto the Sussex countryside.
Quinlan & Francis Terry Architects

OPPOSITE:
The "taxus allee" at Harmony Farm, Greenwich, Connecticut - a harmonious dialog between architecture and landscape design.
Hamady Architects with Doyle Herman Design Associates

PAGE 6:
LONGWOOD FARM (see page 147): The floor of the great room is dropped 2 feet to create a larger volume, while fireplaces at each end anchor the living and dining areas within the larger space.
Curtis & Windham Architects

PAGE 30:
This artisanal studio is filled with a vast library of images and samples, used in designing and creating some of the finest ornamental plaster available.
Foster Reeve & Associates

PAGE 130:
GREEK REVIVAL TOWNHOUSE (see page 157): New Greek Revival Doric columns screen the rooms on the parlor floor.
Franck & Lohsen Architects

PAGE 240:
A pigeonnier (dovecote), designed as a gentleman's cigar bar, acts as a focal point within the landscaped gardens, and references back to the architecture of the new French Colonial Texas house.
Ken Tate Architect

PAGE 256:
A design rendering for a newly created master bedroom in a historic Boston townhouse, complete with furniture and furnishings.
Hamady Architects

REAR COVER:
BOXWOOD (see page 197): A new pergola overlooks the swimming pool and frames multiple views of the house and gardens.
G. P. Schafer Architect

Published in Australia in 2015 by
The Images Publishing Group Pty Ltd
ABN 89 059 734 431
6 Bastow Place, Mulgrave, Victoria 3170, Australia
Tel: +61 3 9561 5544 Fax: +61 3 9561 4860
books@imagespublishing.com
www.imagespublishing.com

Copyright © The Images Publishing Group Pty Ltd 2015
The Images Publishing Group Reference Number: 1127

National Library of Australia Cataloguing-in-Publication entry:

Creator:	Dodd, Phillip James, author.
Title:	An ideal collaboration : the art of classical details II / Phillip James Dodd.
ISBN:	9781864706017 (hardback)
Subjects:	Architecture—Details.
	Architecture, Classical.
	Classicism in architecture.
	Neoclassicism (Architecture)

Dewey Number: 722.8

Printed on 140gsm GoldEast Matt Art paper by Everbest Printing Co. Ltd., in Hong Kong/China

IMAGES has included on its website a page for special notices in relation to this and our other publications. Please visit www.imagespublishing.com.

Every effort has been made to trace the original source of copyright material contained in this book. The publishers would be pleased to hear from copyright holders to rectify any errors or omissions.

The information and illustrations in this publication have been prepared and supplied by the author. While all reasonable efforts have been made to ensure accuracy, the publishers do not, under any circumstances, accept responsibility for errors, omissions and representations express or implied.

Collaboration

Syllabification: col·lab·o·ra·tion

NOUN

1. The action of working with someone to produce or create something.
2. Derived from the Latin term, *collaborare*, translated as "work together".

The Oxford English Dictionary

CONTENTS

This space was completely transformed for the 2014 Kips Bay
Decorator Show House, housed in McKim Mead & White's
historic Villiard Mansion on Madison Avenue.
Cullman & Kravis

Foreword

Ellie Cullman

It gives me great pleasure to participate in Phillip James Dodd's *An Ideal Collaboration: The Art of Classical Details II* – as no subject is more fundamental than collaboration. I have always believed that architecture and interior design can only be successfully realized by close interaction between architect, decorator, and the enormous cast of characters involved, including landscape architects, carpenters, lighting designers, decorative and plain painters, textile designers and upholsterers, and of course, general contractors. The list of industry professionals, who bring their formidable talents to the realization of every project, goes on and on.

I love new projects – getting started is how I imagine it must be when a director begins work on a new film. There is a new script, location, cast, and supporting team. I find it all very exciting and I welcome the help and expertise of the other professionals with whom we work. Even within our office we work in teams, constantly seeking opinions, suggestions, and new ideas from each other for all of our projects. This spirit of collaboration, combined with a deep passion for architecture, has always been one of the guiding principles of our work, as I'm sure is the case for all of the participants featured in this book.

Allan Greenberg, the distinguished architect whom I have been privileged to work with over the years, called this collaboration a "shotgun marriage." Often a client will hire the architect and decorator separately, without carefully reflecting on how the two will interact going forward. This is a critical consideration as a major residence can take two to four years from conception to installation. At every step, a harmonious relationship between the professionals is key and, ultimately, will lead to a much stronger final product. Because every detail must be addressed and analyzed from so many different perspectives, the more talented the architect, the more flexible he or she is in terms of design. Only the insecure are intransigent, unyielding to the considerations of the decorator – or even those of the client!

I always like to reference a moment with Allan, when working on a large and complex house in New Jersey, which was featured in Phillip's previous book *The Art of Classical Details: Theory, Design, and Craftsmanship*. I asked for a specific chair rail height in the family room, as it would work best with the sofa I was proposing. Allan winked, leaned over the conference table and exclaimed in his elegant South African accent, "Your wish is my command."

Our design mantra was crystallized from then on and has stayed constant. Never draw a line between architecture and decoration – they must work in tandem, unquestionably. There is simply no good decorating without good architecture; the "good bones" that make the decorator's work soar. Choices we make about the furniture, fabrics, and finishes must be carefully based on the rhythm and logic of the architectural elements of each interior. Chair rail heights DO matter!

Whenever we decorate, our goal is to create a harmonious entity. By unifying the architectural vocabulary and the primary decorative elements, we ensure that every finished project is completely cohesive, not just within each room, but also from room to room. In fact, we shy away from projects requiring us to decorate only a room or two because if some rooms are already completed, we can't work them into the rest of the house in a meaningful way. I imagine that the same can be said for the role of landscape architect, where often the architecture is the backdrop to the gardens. All of these collaborative connections are absolutely necessary for the end result to have an elegant flow.

Personally, I am so grateful for the magnificent spaces created by the wonderful architects I have worked with over the years. Many whose work is featured in this book: Mark Appleton, Allan Greenberg, Ike Kligerman Barkley, John Murray, Jeffrey Smith, Dinyar Wadia, and Peter Zimmerman among others.

We are so lucky to have Phillip bring us the collaborative efforts of so many talented and world-class architects. Each of their stories reflects not just the relationship of architect to decorator, but also the critical component of the additional voices on every project. This unique insight into the role of architect, decorator, landscape architect, vendor, craftsman, artist, and teacher allows us to understand and appreciate the broader picture. Understanding the dynamic nature of collaboration is key to discerning what makes a successful project.

The fact is that none of us works in a vacuum. The fully articulated and realized projects in this book – made visible by the accompanying photos and essays – are a testament to the mutual respect we support and maintain in this close-knit, highly spirited, and very collaborative business of design.

The living room of a historic John Volk designed home in Palm Beach, is at once rustic and opulent. Traditional materials and neutral tones from the original pecky cypress ceiling and stuccoed walls are juxtaposed with fresh, vibrant and varied furnishings.
Cullan & Kravis

Inspired by the film *Some Like It Hot*, this bedroom from the 2014 Kips Bay Decorator Show House has copper and aluminum leaf as the base color, rather than paint. Lacquered furniture and contemporary artwork refresh the otherwise traditional paneled room.
Cullman & Kravis

CREOLE COLONIAL (see page 213): Viewed from across a pond, the mass of the house is divided among several structures, blending several local architectural styles.
Ken Tate Architect

Introduction

"I don't intend to build in order to have clients. I intend to have clients in order to build."
Howard Roark, protagonist of Ayn Rand's *The Fountainhead*

The romanticized notion of the architect as a lone genius has existed ever since the Italian Renaissance, when Giorgio Vasari first published his biography of the great painters, sculptors, and architects of the day. Here Vasari popularized the myth that all artists—and architects in particular—were chosen by and endowed by God. Fast-forward almost four centuries to 1943, and it is no mere coincidence that Ayn Rand would cast the protagonist of her seminal work *The Fountainhead*—an individual genius with innate creativity and God-given talent—as an architect.

Not surprisingly, Howard Roark—Ayn Rand's fictional architect—was modeled after no other than Frank Lloyd Wright. Universally lauded as a genius, and worshipped by all, the *American Institute of Architects* named Wright "The greatest American architect of all time". Yet not all of his clients felt the same way. One described him as "egotistical, overbearing, and arrogant", and another, when complaining that his roof was leaking on the dining table was simply told to "move the table". The price of hiring the services of genius? A giant-sized ego accompanied by wet furniture.

Between them, Howard Roark and Frank Lloyd Wright—America's most famous fictional and real-life architects—have reinforced the widely held perception of the architect as the lone egotistical artistic genius; that they exist not to serve, but to be served; that they, and they alone, are responsible for every single aspect of a design; and that the client should feel privileged to live in one of their creations.

However, in today's modern dynamic environment, with an increased specialization in services, we are constantly being told that collaboration and teamwork skills are critical. No longer is it about how much one person happens to know, as one person simply can't know everything. In the age of Google and corporate team-building

ABOVE:
A custom design wrought iron gate frames the view from the house, through the formal gardens to the landscape beyond.
D. Stanley Dixon Architect

OPPOSITE:
The design rendering of this new Anglo-Caribbean style home in Palm Beach, Florida, shows careful research into historic precedents of classical architecture in the South. The design amalgamates influences from Charleston Colonial, tropical British Colonial Revival architecture, and French Caribbean and Creole - with hints of Jefferson's pavilion designs at the University of Virginia.

retreats, the collective is lauded over the individual. We are told that the best solutions emerge from the process of sharing ideas, and engaging in an interactive dialogue. That a kinetic process feeds creative thought, and that group problem-solving exercises result in a better overall outcome. The term "collaboration" has become a catch-phrase, along with words such as preparation, motivation, interpretation, communication, and implementation.

And yet amongst this backdrop of modern-day business rhetoric, true collaborative relationships in architecture and design remain relatively rare. This is in part due to the traditional emphasis on individual creation, where each designer is more often than not focused on their own individual objectives, unable to transcend their own egos, and unwilling to relinquish sole authorship—in the fear that their voice and design intent should become diluted. Sadly, relationships between designers working on the same project are more likely to be combative and competitive, rather than collaborative.

We can trace this inability to share, as well as the adversarial attitude, back to the very beginning of an architect's training. Despite working in communal studios, the typical student's architectural education is a lone and solitary enterprise. Rarely are there group or interdisciplinary projects. Never are there clients. Instead the student engages in a sole creation, the culmination of which is the jury review. Here the student takes an argumentative position, taught to passionately and fiercely defend their designs in a competitive and combative environment. No wonder when entering the workplace the architect feels that all aspects of the design should fall under their jurisdiction. They are merely reverting back to their training—or lack of it.

This traditional role of an architect is one that is held dear to the hearts of the architectural establishment. That is not to say that they don't recognize the inevitable erosion of that role, as an increased complexity in design and construction has demanded a division of labor into a far more focused and specialized skill set. Instead they just choose to ignore it, in the fear that it may dilute the importance of their self-revered profession.

Why is this? Well, in part it goes back to the definition of the word *architect*. Derived from the Latin *architectus*, which in turn comes from the Greek *architeckton* (architect literally translates as "master-builder"). The first record of the term being used is in reference to Imhotep, architect to the Egyptian Pharoah Djoser (2670 BC). Imhotep was considered a creative and intellectual genius, and in return received special privileges from the royal family, earning the titles of chief engineer, prime minister, crown prince, and head of the royal court before being raised to the level of a deity two thousand years after his death. This is of course not a fair comparison, though many of today's architects and designers may feel that they also deserve this level of recognition! But in this day and age architects are not master-builders (nor are they decorators or landscape architects) and in order to realize their ideas they need to collaborate and interact with an enormous cast of professionals. Architecture in the 21st century is complex—although it should never be complicated—and requires many interdisciplinary relationships in order to be successfully executed. The world has changed since the time of Imhotep, and so, too, has the role of the architect.

That is not to say that the architect's duties have become diminished, although some (in particular interior designers, builders, and client reps) have looked to capitalize on the situation by marginalizing the role of the architect, and elevating their own importance and workload. Increasingly interior designers have looked to take control of everything on the inside of the house, asking the architect to provide them a blank canvas for their creation. Likewise many builders are frustrated architects, and take a certain pride in making design decisions on the spot, not realizing the negative knock-on effect that these ill-thought decisions will inevitably lead to. The client rep is a relatively new occupation, and an invaluable one, especially when the homeowner is not able to meet or communicate with the architect on a regular basis. Not content with the role of the clients' lieutenant and confident, many client reps look to seize the role of the project manager away from the architect. All told it is now the equivalent of a creative free-for-all, with other professionals claiming a larger slice of the pie that once solely belonged to the architect, while in the process claiming that this division of responsibilities benefits the homeowner and the overall design.

And so in a relatively short space of time we have gone from the individual egotistical genius unwilling to share, to a group of insecure individuals, each aiming to one-up the other, and hoping that he or she who shouts loudest (figuratively and metaphorically) will garner the spoils. This is not collaboration, nor sadly is it a solution to the division of labor that has necessitated the involvement of many hands.

ABOVE:
A Tribute to Charles Robert Cockerell, RA: Part of a capriccio depicting the total work of the seminal English architect.
Oil on Canvas by Carl Laubin

OPPOSITE:
Originally design by Robert Adam, this London townhouse located in Fitzroy Square, was later converted for hospital use loosing much of its detail. The building has now been remodeled again for residential use - designed and decorated to reference all of its past while also remaining contemporary (as shown here at the old service staircase and landing).
Russell Taylor

An Ideal Collaboration refutes the notion that the best designs come from a lone designer, and dispels the stereotype that all architects and designers are incapable of playing well with others.

As with *The Art of Classical Details*, this book examines some of the finest examples of contemporary classical architecture—focusing on their use of materials, intricate detailing, and exquisite craftsmanship—and, as before is divided into two distinct chapters, *The Essays* and *The Projects*. Enlisting the support of 16 influential members of the design community, each of their essays explain the importance of collaboration within their own disciplines, while also referencing the relationships that go towards creating a successful outcome for all. *The Projects* then presents an illustrated look at 22 of today's finest classically designed homes. Employing the invaluable guidance prescribed in the writings of the first chapter, this portfolio of contemporary buildings exhibits the work of some of the most recognizable and celebrated architects in the United States and Great Britain.

It is worth noting that the material in this book is not meant as an exemplar or building companion, providing precise rules for designers to follow. Rather, it is a survey of current classical architecture, where we are able to read, observe, and understand, the pivotal role that architects, interior designers and decorators, landscape architects, consultants, builders, craftspeople, artists, manufacturers, vendors and scholars all play in contemporary classical design, and in creating timeless cohesive architecture.

Whether it be *design in isolation, or design by committee*, both approaches only dilute, complicate, and confuse the outcome. Inevitably they are destined for failure. Great architecture is the result of a combined effort, and the result of many individual hands. Yet there needs to be a shared vision and the recognition that someone—more often than not, the architect—is at the helm. Most importantly, an ideal collaboration requires an understanding, and an appreciation, of the role that all parties play in the design and construction of a home. To arbitrarily assign people to a design team is not necessarily going to lead to a successful collaboration. Ideally you want to find colleagues whose work you admire, trust and respect, and then try to establish a working relationship that you can cultivate over a long and fruitful period of time. Successful collaboration, just like great architecture, is not easy, and as the following pages show, *An Ideal Collaboration* is truly an art form.

OPPOSITE:
BOXWOOD (see page 197): This bespoke wood fireplace, with dog-leg jambs and a semi-barrel frieze, is designed as part as part of an overall paneled wall composition.
G. P. Schafer Architect

ABOVE:
A CLASSICAL TOWNHOUSE (see page 179): The success of this fireplace is due to the selection of rich materials with contrasting colors, with obsidian (black) lacquered wall panels and an antique Sienna marble, set off with a white trim.
S. R. Gambrell with Liederbach & Graham Architects

ABOVE:
BOXWOOD (see page 197): A detail of the hand-gouged oak paneling in the library, which gives a contemporary spin on an otherwise traditional room.
G. P. Schafer Architect

OPPOSITE:
A CLASSICAL REVIVAL TOWNHOUSE (see page 203): Looking down on an elegant staircase that spirals through three floors of the townhouse, and is illuminated by a three-part chandelier and a circular skylight above.
Andrew Skurman Architects

OPPOSITE:
Subtle details such as the beaded clapboard, window surround, operable shutters, and a monotone color palette. Simple yet not simplistic.

Andrew Skurman Architects

ABOVE:
A NEW FRAMHOUSE (see page 191): The entrance hall includes a stair balustrade that terminates in a scroll, and random-width reclaimed pine flooring - faux-painted to mimic marble.

John B. Murray Architect

ABOVE:
DREAMING A HOUSE (see page 33): A stucco vaulted ceiling and limestone columns and pilasters, at the entrance of this Mediterranean Revival style home in New Orleans.
Ken Tate Architect

OPPOSITE:
A design rendering by Francis Terry for an ornamental plaster ceiling at Kilboy, County Tipperary, Ireland.
Quinlan & Francis Terry Architects

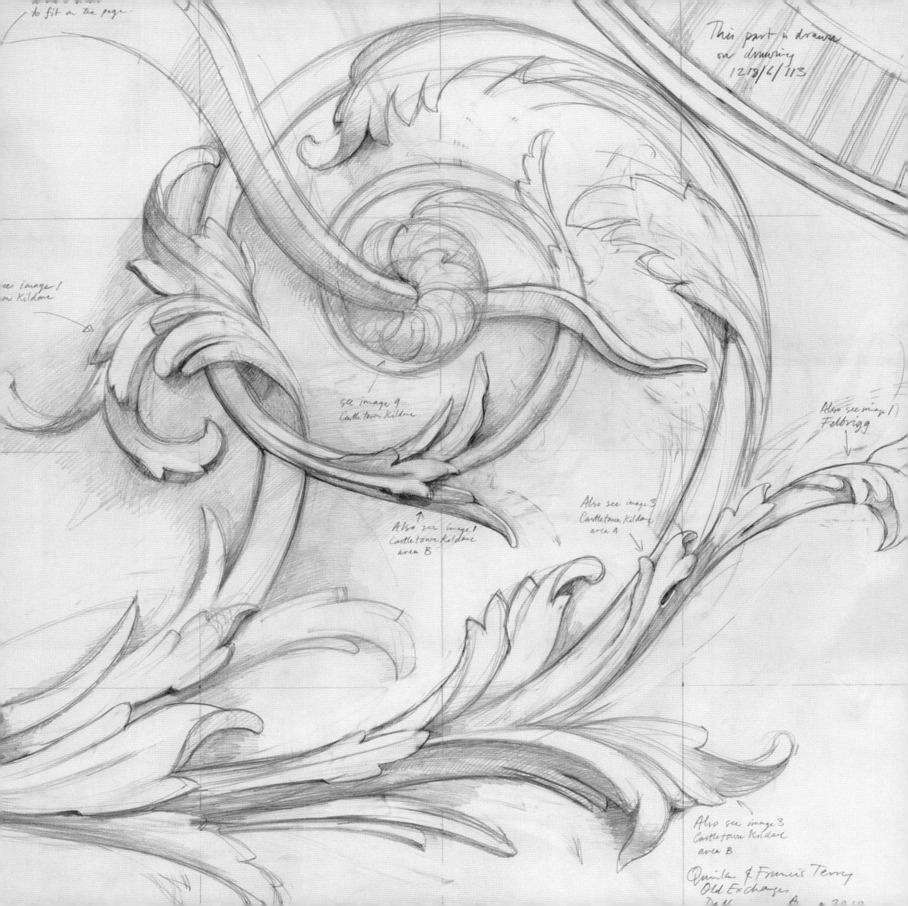

to fit on the page.

This part is drawn on drawing 1213/6/113

see image 1 on Kildare

see image 9 Castletown Kildare

Also see image 1 Felbrigg

Also see image 1 Castletown Kildare area B

Also see image 3 Castletown Kildare area A

Also see image 3 Castletown Kildare area B

Quinlan & Francis Terry Old Exchanges

PART I

THE ESSAYS

Photographed while still under construction, facing St. Charles Avenue is a single-story portico with a row of arches supported by cut stone columns that is reminiscent of the work of Palladio in Vicenza.
Ken Tate Architect

Dreaming a House

Ken Tate with Susan Sully

When the client comes to an architect, they are usually following a dream— often a vague dream of living a life of health, abundance, and happiness that has not yet coalesced into any specific imagery. The architect's job is to dream their house into existence, pulling it into three-dimensional reality through a process of experiential imagining. This process involves long periods of walking through rooms that don't exist, gradually envisioning how they are viewed one from the other, how light shapes their spaces, and what it feels like to be in them. This visualizing is a layered process that begins with the massing of the building, proceeding to an understanding of its functional circulation, and progressively arrives at the level of specific architectural devices. In the best projects, the key people involved contribute their own vision to this dreaming, but also understand that they must surrender something to it, trusting the dream to have a life of its own. When this happens, the design unfolds successively and intuitively, culminating in a final result that is both surprising and instantly recognizable as just the way it should be.

The renderings featured here are among more than 280 pages of drawings created during the design of the Jeffrey and Walton Goldring residence on St. Charles Avenue in New Orleans. An invitation to design a new residence on St. Charles Avenue is a dream commission for any architect inspired by classical architecture, but also a daunting one. In this case, one of the biggest challenges was the complex permission procedure required to remove the existing house, despite a strict moratorium on demolition. This was led by New Orleans native and architect Dennis Brady, who not only has a deep understanding of the city's architectural history, but also resides on the side street defining the corner lot where the new house was to be built. While we waited for permission to be granted, my clients and I immersed ourselves in the architectural context of the area, a neighborhood known as Uptown settled in the late 19th and early 20th centuries during the period now known as the Colonial Revival.

We began our research by driving along St. Charles Avenue and its many beautiful cross streets, as well as the gated boulevard of Audubon Place, established in the early 1900s, where some of the neighborhood's most impressive houses stand. Although, initially, the clients had proposed the French Classical aesthetic, our observations soon directed us to Italian, Mediterranean, and Spanish Colonial styles. The new house needed to be a timeless, classical house to complement its St. Charles Avenue setting, but also a comfortable one for a young couple planning to raise a family. The French Classical house can easily become high style, particularly in an urban setting, and this more romantic language seemed better suited to the way the clients wanted to live.

Considering the parameters and architectural context of the corner site, I determined that the house needed to have a formal, two-story façade on St. Charles Avenue and a less formal, asymmetrical presence on the side street. Beginning to flesh out this idea, I envisioned a broad, symmetrical main mass facing the avenue with two single-story wings stretching behind to embrace a large, private courtyard. But something was still missing. The house needed an architectural element to facilitate the shift from the classical two-story façade to the more casual side elevations. What came to mind was something unexpected and even whimsical—a three-story tower like the very romantic ones found in the Mediterranean Revival houses of Palm Beach, Coral Gables, Bel Air, and Santa Barbara. Although this tower would have no functional purpose, it solved the problem by synthesizing the parts of the house into a harmonious whole.

As my focus shifted to the selection of specific architectural devices, I considered Palladio's work in the Veneto, Francis Burrall Hoffman's Vizcaya in Miami, Addison Mizner's and Maurice Fatio's mansions in Palm Beach, and Wallace Neff's and George Washington Smith's Mediterranean Revival villas in California. I was channeling Palladio as I envisioned the face of the house, but I felt that his characteristic pediment-over-portico would be out of character with the neighboring dwellings, many of which have second-story terraces for watching the parades. Inspired instead by his façade for the Basilica in Vicenza, I designed a single-story portico with a row of arches supported by cut stone columns that forms a deep, colonnaded gallery on the ground floor and a stone balustrade terrace above. Although many of the

portico's details, including the carved rondels over the flanking shoulders of the arches—quote the Basilica—the proportions are reduced to a domestic scale. Combined with the overall simplicity of the façade's remaining architecture, the effect is distinctive and enticing, strong enough to carry an important house on a corner lot, but without shouting.

On the rear of the main mass, an iconic Palladian pediment-over-portico carries the formality of the primary façade around to the back and provides the opportunity for a spacious loggia. For the wings paralleling the courtyard, however, I tapped into the American interpretation of Italian and Spanish architecture popularized during the early decades of the Mediterranean Revival. The picturesque quality of the iron gates and second-story pergola above the side entrance, the pergola terminating one of the wings, and the tower, which is visible from the courtyard, all capture the romance of that era. When I first introduced the idea of the tower to the clients, I could tell they weren't completely convinced about it, but ultimately, it became one of their favorite aspects of the design. They bought into my dream even when they couldn't fully comprehend it, acting with the kind of courage that allows an architect to follow wherever the vision leads. This is what makes for a great collaboration.

The next stage involved intensive conversations with a larger team of participants, including the Goldrings' art adviser, New Orleans-based art dealer Arthur Rogers. The clients, whose family foundation is a major contributor to the Ogden Museum of Southern Art, wanted the villa to house their growing collection of paintings and sculpture. Meeting with Rogers and interior designer Gerrie Bremmerman, we reviewed every piece in their art inventory, some of them quite large, in order to devise the perfect spot for each. This allowed the designer to select her furnishings accordingly, whether to harmonize or juxtapose with the art in each room, and informed lighting design customized with the art in mind.

Because many works in the Goldrings' collection are contemporary and colorful, Gerrie and I simultaneously realized that the house itself needed to be neutral, especially where art was to occur. Envisioning the rooms, I saw walls expressed in unadorned, smooth plaster except in the main stair hall, where rusticated blocks of the Texas limestone used on the exterior would be employed. With simple casings at the openings and in some places no casings at all, the plain plaster walls called for more adorned ceilings—groin vaults, paneling, antique wood beams, barrel vaults, and large coved ceilings.

I began dreaming a ceiling treatment for the living room with limed double oak beams supported by classically carved oak brackets repeated at large intervals with oak purlins between. The oak would be reclaimed antique material and the brackets crafted by renowned master woodcarver Frederick Wilbur. Once my head designer and perspective renderer John Gaudet drew the ceiling along with chevron-patterned oak flooring and an Italian carved stone mantle, copied after an Istrian stone mantle by Palladio, I knew this was what I was looking for. When the clients and their interior designer saw the rendering, we were on the same page, literally and figuratively.

The one missing piece of the completed vision was the landscape design. In order to integrate the house with its site, the plantings needed to be Mediterranean in character—formal in the front and more romantic behind. Gavin Duke of Page/Duke Landscape Architects, who has a classical voice, joined the team, articulating colorful plantings, the placement of Royal Palms in the courtyard, and designing terracotta pots and stone planters.

During the lengthy design process (as of this writing, with the house already three years under construction, we are still drawing details), Jeffrey Goldring called frequently to ask what I was doing. Once I replied, "I'm dreaming your house," which most accurately describes the architect's way of getting to the truth of any design. In the field of architecture, there has to be someone who carries the entire house within himself or herself as it moves along, saying yea or nay when something seems out of place. In this case, the clients always sought my opinion about whatever was being added to the mix—lighting, indoor and outdoor furniture, curtains, and plantings. This is an unusual trait for a young couple that has never built a house before—the understanding that there is a holistic quality to the design and construction. In order for a house to transcend the egos of all parties involved and to be important, timeless, and perfect (perhaps in an "imperfect" way), it needs to be channeled through the spirit of the architect, while touching the souls of all who use and love it. ❧

A computer rendering of the new home as seen from St. Charles Avenue in Garden District, complete with a streetcar in the foreground, that captures the charm of romance of the City of New Orleans.
Ken Tate Architect

BLACK & WHITE HOUSE (see page 169): The unusual, and bold, choice of black shingles and board-and-batten siding with white trim was inspired by a historic Swedish barn with a similar color palette.
Ike Kligerman Barkley Architects

Learning to Share

Joel Barkley

I have a useful childhood memory that illustrates the value of collaboration. I remember spreading out on the floor as a seven-year-old with my beloved set of Lego blocks, and building a well-thought-out modernist white "townhouse" on exactly half of the toy's green plastic base. Beforehand, I had sorted the blocks by color and shape, and carefully fitted together a well-proportioned, rigorously detailed house with clearly formed windows, doors, openings and even a modern corner fireplace. My best friend David joined me to play, and I had left half of the Lego base empty for him to build his own adjacent version. I completed my half before he arrived, in order to show him my good taste and skills at building. But when he started to build, he didn't pay much attention to my example. He didn't sort his materials by color or shape. He just dove in, vigorously attaching unmatched blocks into a fantastic and irrational Dionysian assemblage. At first, I remember being annoyed by his approach, but as I let my guard down and really looked, I found myself in awe of his sublime construction, almost Piranesi-like in its potential vastness and complexity. That afternoon, I spent much more time dwelling mentally in his half than mine, adapting some of David's ideas into my half, reordering the whole into something of a unified masterpiece.

As I mature as an architect, it is clear to me now how critical collaboration is. Architects tend to overthink things and I firmly believe that it is collaboration, as well as the conscious withholding of judgment of counterintuitive ideas, that give an essential spark to our firm's work. The most important collaborator on a house is, of course, the owner. Their experience and perspective is always a new one, regardless of how hands-on they are in the design. For me, the relationship between the architect and the interior designer is almost as important.

Constantly, I learn from the humanist, "from within" approach of most interior designers. At first, it was often a challenge to my academically fed, youthful arrogance for an interior designer or decorator to teach me, somewhat remedially, that a human might want to feel centered in a space or know where the front door should be. It can be humbling, an interior designer's insistence that we proportion a living room to accommodate a full-sized sofa facing the right way, or to ensure that curtains have a place to go when drawn.

My architectural priorities are naturally formal and spatial. I love creating dramatic turns, long visual axes, and framed views. I am keenly aware of exterior forces on the plan of a house, from without, such as the surrounding landscape and the movement of the sun. Add to this, the interior designer's focus of the more personal, tactile details—the feel, the texture, even the smell of the room—and we always have something bigger than the both of us.

When working with the best interior designers and decorators, I've learned to withhold my judgment in the face of ideas that initially go against what I envision. This can be a real challenge and a face-reddening test of ego. "Are you sure you want double doors leading into a bedroom?" one brilliant collaborating interior designer asked me recently. I recalled that I'd never designed double doors for a bedroom. I agreed they can seem grandiose or pretentious and can be awkward to operate. However, in this context—a gut renovation of a well-detailed Norman Revival house from 1927, I had purposely left original doors on axis with original French doors to a terrace opposite. I was excited about trying a bit of formal opulence that I normally would have eschewed. I confess that as of this writing I am still easing into the reality of a less grand room, but with the confidence that the interior designer's push-back will open up a whole new character for the room that I can't see yet. Perhaps he is coyly making more empty wall space in the bedroom for a very important work of art.

A good collaborator entertains suggestions that may seem wrong at first. If you are able to hold your tongue and truly listen, the wisdom of another perspective can enliven a rigidly "correct" design, loading it with more layers of thought and experience in a way that nothing short of another human mind can do. Pure *auteurship* is an intense and lonely process. While nothing could or should spare an architect the splendid isolation of hours alone bent over their lonely drafting board, we have to re-enter the world for our visions to be realized, and our ideal plans need to be tested by talented people with different points of view.

I often joke that we'll use an idea from anyone as long as it is the best one in the room—and as long as I can take the credit for it in the end. The whole battery of collaborators has a voice—general contractors, landscape architects, lighting designers, structural engineers, stone masons, woodworkers, vendors, etc. Technologically, architecture has gone beyond anything that one person can know. I don't know everything, but I certainly know whom to ask. This is true for design also, I don't keep current with all aspects of design, and I need others to contribute their experiences from their respective realms. The truth is, it is always a credit to everyone at the table to be part of a project that benefits from open sharing and listening. There is an invested energy all around the table at the naissance of something that everyone has a hand in making.

The black and white house in this book I did with Alexa Hampton. Alexa draws all the time and when I first met her years ago at a dinner, we sat together taking turns at adding to a napkin sketch, an "exquisite corpse" of sorts that developed from new thoughts added to old, a constant adaptation to previous moves and intentions.

Little did we know at the time that we would be collaborating in a similar fashion on this family house in Greenwich, Connecticut. At our first meeting, she called my black wood and white stucco design "an Oreo." Her playful jab took me aback (I can be sensitive) but Alexa was starting this back-and-forth dialog between expressive color and the *Gestalt* black and white exterior of the house that I'd brought to the table. The result is a stylish,

BLACK & WHITE HOUSE (see page 169): Decorator Alexa Hampton created rooms that are a casual but sophisticated counterpoint to the black-and-white exterior.
Ike Kligerman Barkley Architects

BLACK & WHITE HOUSE (see page 169): Dubbed *Svenglish* by architect Joel Barkley, the home is a blend of traditional American shingle architecture, English arts and crafts, and Swedish charm.
Ike Kligerman Barkley Architects

Tucked under the window in the kitchen is a small breakfast area. Decorator Alexa Hampton adds a bold splash of orange at the built-in banquette, window valance, and even the cookware, to off-set the soothing Swedish blues that are used elsewhere in the house.

compelling, family house that absolutely glows from the inside. It couldn't have developed without her taking her turn, without the iterative process of one designer riffing off of the intention of the other, of successive moves that create something neither of us alone could have predicted. It was a project that was able to grow between minds—kind of like the Lego house David and I built so many years ago.

As a young architect I knew it all and couldn't wait to get it all on paper, not knowing when the next design opportunity would come. Now that I have many projects under my belt, I know that there will be a next house, another chance to try some spatial tweak that has me preoccupied. I also have a self-confidence that leaves me open and thirsty for the ideas of others. Looking back at our best houses, they all came about through collaboration, by sharing, by playing well with others, and by having fun. ❧

A CLASSICAL TOWNHOUSE (see page 179): The walls of the Library in this Chicago Townhouse are finished in a custom peacock-blue lacquer.
S. R. Gambrell with Liederbach & Graham Architects

The Alchemy of Good Design

Steven Gambrel

The most successful projects begin with a creative, brave, and determined client. Ideally the architectural firm is committed to classic proportion and layered materiality, and is well versed in vernacular precedence. As a team, we set forth a program for the house, ideally one that will settle softly within its contextual environment, while suiting the demands of a modern family and unique client requirements.

After reviewing initial plans and elevations provided by the architect, I consider the influences that have led the team to this scheme thus far, and start researching visual references that might enhance the drawings in order to make the rooms speak their own language. Having studied architecture at the University of Virginia, my knowledge of the field is such that I can layer multiple references and sketches on to the initial plans and elevations. My architectural background also allows me to fully understand scale, which enables the interior detailing to meld seamlessly with the architecture of the volumes and the exterior. I am not beholden to a particular style or period, instead, I choose from centuries of common themes, often going back to earlier examples of a chosen architectural style. Usually the more peculiar examples found in history are the ones I am attracted to—often they lead to the best inspiration. I print out images of endless details either photographed by me on countless trips to museums, villages, and great houses and monuments of the past, or I include images gathered from books on subjects as diverse as Georgian architecture, Abstract Expressionism, and French 20th-century furniture.

We meet with the architectural firm and we discuss the plans and elevations and enthusiastically agree that many of the references are indeed shared references. It is uncanny how many times a book's pages will be marked with the same ceiling detail, or favorite paneled room, by both the architect and the decorator. Often the images and details that we reference are from 20th-century houses by American classicists such as David Adler or H.T. Lindeberg. There is something very tangible about learning from 20th-century adaptations of classical structures; perhaps it is the freedom of architectural language and the sparse use of ornamentation that feel more appropriate to our work. Certainly the plans and sequence of rooms seem more appropriate to the modern way one inhabits spaces.

During the process of developing the drawings and overall style of the house, I spend more time with the clients, and together we discover a unique vocabulary that layers their personality onto the plans and elevations. We discuss their lifestyle, visit their current residence for more clues about the day-to-day, and determine the idiosyncrasies of their routine. Samples of materials and images from inspirational rooms start to fill my worktable, as I share my thoughts about the evolving interiors and their relationship to the exterior and nature. The orientation of the sun provides natural clues as to which parts of the house want to be layered and cozy, and which parts want to have large, ample space with leaner millwork details, ideally flooded with sunlight and reflection. Textiles, wall surfaces, and samples of millwork help inform my descriptions of the contrasting rooms. Rich deep tones are often layered with paneled wall details, bookcases, patterns, and elaborate ceilings, while the brighter rooms have chalky colors, crisp walls and smoother surfaces, often leaving room for art and light to fill the void.

After the team feels confident that the general scheme has developed successfully, details start to unfold. I understand all of the components added when color, decorative surfaces, and furnishings are installed at the very end of the project. The samples of stone, flooring, plaster, millwork, and cabinetry are all just elements to support the overall spirit of the place; slight adjustments can change the predominant tone. Furniture plans are prepared and presented along with textiles and furniture styles for each room. These schemes are always delivered along with elevations, wall finishes, mantle details and millwork, so that the client and architect can visualize the completed project. Furniture plans and storyboards are also required so that the architect and decorator can collaborate on reflected ceiling plans for lighting, locations of technology and scale of furnishings. I refer back to the elevations and plans continuously throughout a project, to confirm that the scale of furniture, artwork, and lighting is ideal for the space.

Paneling details are often slightly modified in the drawing phase as one finds unusual vintage fixtures, artwork, hardware details, or adjusts the wall finishes during the decorating process. Ultimately, this level of open collaboration between the two firms results in interiors that appear effortless and evolved, not stiff or one-dimensional.

I see my overall contribution as one of editing, which seems counter to the job description. It is my job to balance materials and determine the complexity of the finishes included in the construction of the interiors. Recently, when collaborating on a large new house being built in Chicago, I had the good fortune to work with Phil Liederbach, of Liederbach and Graham Architects. Drawings of the house were influenced by exceptional examples of Classical houses built in the 1920s to 1940s, in Chicago. The details were not only scaled beautifully but referenced the local history of a culturally rich region. However, I had collaborated with the client on her desire for a very personal decorating scheme and this led to adjustments to the proposed finishes. The library changed from a suggested wood finish, most commonly seen in houses of this stature, to a highly polished peacock lacquer. While elaborate paneling on the drawings of the hallway walls were reduced to a chair rail, to allow for a lean pale gray-blue waxed artisan's plaster finish, with room for art. The barrel-vaulted ceiling of a smaller sitting room became a glossy amber glow, while the kitchen developed with materials of wired oak, softly reflective glazed tiles, and rough-coat plaster walls. Unconventional lighting, both vintage and custom, were chosen to contrast with the very stylish, yet highly appropriate mantelpieces and casing details of the public spaces.

A CLASSICAL TOWNHOUSE (see page 179): The entrance hall as seen from the second floor. The black-and-white marble floor, vivid red carpet, and custom designed chandelier all combine to create a sophisticated aesthetic, reminiscent of the 1940's.
S. R. Grambrell with Liederbach & Graham Architects

A CLASSICAL TOWNHOUSE (see page 179): The living room a
medley of rich materials and color choices, including American
walnut wall paneling, and a vaulted ceiling.
S. R. Grambrell with Liederbach & Graham Architects

Featuring a tiled barrel-vaulted ceiling, rough-coat plaster walls, oversized vintage iron lanterns, and decorated with Andy Warhol prints, the design is a fresh take on the great service kitchens of the past.

The installation phase of the project is the most exciting phase, as the final chapter is revealed, and the architect and decorator can observe how meticulously designed architectural details blend seamlessly with a collection of furnishings ranging from the 18th to 21st centuries. The applied color palette, surface patterns, wood finishes, and textiles balance the scale of the rooms, and prepare the house for the lifestyle of the client to unfold. As the rooms are carefully furnished and styled with objects to reinforce the color palette and characteristics of the space, they take on a life of their own and, ultimately, appear to have been there for generations, only adapted and refreshed along the way.

After the installation is complete, the evidence of dozens of drawings, many assistants and artisans, and months of construction that it took to create the space, disappear into a complete wholeness, where only the client can fully appreciate the efforts put forth in the ideal collaboration. ❧

Donald Kaufman mixing colors in his Manhattan Studio.
Donald Kaufman Color

Collaboration in Color

Donald Kaufman

I like to think that architecture is about drawing energy into living spaces and that light, through the shaping of forms, can be captured and manipulated to align with our sensibilities and enhance our existence.

For centuries, architects have sought to create physical structures filled with animated illumination. To accomplish this, they have shaped openings in structures for light to enter and interact with the surroundings—playing off multicolored particles of marble and stone, skittering along interlaced grains in wood, circulating through sheets of translucent glazes, and flowing across variegated textures of tinted plaster.

Because this endlessly rebounding radiance is color-coded, we not only see it as the hue of the enclosure, but we also feel it as what the anthropologist Michael Taussig has called a *polymorphous magical substance*. We grasp its qualities through the shock of contrast, as when we step out of a warmly lit house into an icy cold twilight.

Working as a house painter, I had been using standard colors straight from the can, but inevitably found myself making alterations to fit each situation. Gradually, I began to recognize that my back-and-forth pigment adjustments were creating the shimmering atmospheres on walls that I experienced in nature. A San Francisco architect, David Robinson, first noticed the paint's special play with light and asked to use it on a project.

Although I had appreciated the potential of these mixes, it wasn't until this first collaboration that I understood how much teamwork and communication would be required to make the evanescence concrete. Owing to often intense emotions that accompany color choices, vagaries of vision and language, and the difficulties in transposing intensities from small chips to large surfaces, we found that architects, designers, and clients, though committed to achieving rare beauty and function, often floundered when trying to agree on specifics. Enter the color consultants.

Luckily, the architects who began to hire us became invested in our mutual success. Most hadn't realized that in using standard paint, they were depending on products that had, since the 1940s, been sacrificing rich pigmentation for lower costs. This gradual attrition of aesthetics was based on the manufacturers' mistaken notions that different coatings should compete on durability, ease of application, and better hiding—but not on better quality, higher performing color. Beige or gray, trendy or retro, all were thought to have (or lack) the same flair and depth. As a result, industrial paint making—replacing hand-mixed paint with pre-programmed spectrophotometers—was gradually killing the aesthetic potential of architectural color. One of the many small paint companies, long gone since the 1950s, advertised that its paints had "more pigments than are needed to make the color." Liberty Paint Company had known the secret to making paint colors rich.

Ironically, this standardization is what put us in business. It was also the catalyst for our architectural education, since the architects, who were themselves sophisticated in color, made sure we understood the logic of their constructions and how our palettes would complement their ordering of forms and contribute to the fulfillment of their visions.

Our first New York apartment collaboration, with Charles Gwathmey, started with a cool greeting and a rather perfect lecture on the relation of values (lights to darks) with hierarchies of supports and planes. Since our visual system evolved to distinguish lighter from darker, long before becoming sensitive to the differences between red and green, this essential instruction became our template for other projects regardless of their style.

As our collaborations progressed, Taffy Dahl, my wife and design partner noticed that clients regularly brought us in as referees. Architects were asking us to explain how our colors and their arrangements throughout the spaces would augment the overall flow and elegance of their design. It became apparent that, in addition to colors, identities were also at stake. Our strategy for untangling these issues involved asking all concerned parties one question. What self-image do you want your house to project? The question originated from a bit of family lore. One cousin, whenever told by a friend that he or she was going to a party, asked, what are you going as? Clients work to express their individuality and architects struggle to finesse these identifiers into practical concerns of siting, style, and budget, all critical components of a coherent outcome.

Working in this realm, our challenge has been to uncover common goals while grappling with the reality that we humans see differently from one another. It is the backlog of all we have seen that shapes what we now see. Our eyes are not cameras recording continuous videos but are receptors sending radiant energy to our brains for interpretation, and then arranging this energy according to our conscious and unconscious priorities. Each of us uses these collected sensations to create the worlds we alone see.

Additionally, evolution has structured our vision to form stable pictures and is very resistant to incorporating even the slightest bit of new information. Despite this, colors can generate visual illusions. Brightness, for example, can be brought into a dark space by borrowing from one of the most common sights in the natural landscape—shadow. On the brightest days, sun and shade exhibit the sharpest contrasts. When we use the same starkly divided values in a gloomy space, our vision recreates, indoors, the bright outdoor light.

Each individual values in a gloomy space, our vision recreates, indoors, the bright outdoor light. incorporating even the slightest bit of new information. Despite this, colors cancolors and finishes in the right place, under the right lighting, and at the right moment, more consensus can be had in two minutes of looking than in many hours of talking around a conference table. For exteriors we have assembled entire corners of houses, showing how shingle, stone, windows, and glass abut and then mounting the simulation on a forklift to catch the light from all directions of the compass. Mock-

"Nature is the ultimate source of every color palette – moss green, saffron yellow, cherry red. It seems impossible to image the hue without thinking of something in nature that expresses its character. The color seems to be the soul of that plant, that flower, and that stone." – Donald Kaufman

To facilitate selecting and organizing palettes, large format color cards are presented in archival boxes, allowing for new colors to be easily added.
Donald Kaufman Color

ups for interiors need not be so elaborate. We have often decided on a palette by throwing small pieces of wood, tile, and fabrics into a pile.

On many occasions, we have maneuvered around visual preconceptions by calling attention to colors close at hand. The color for a barn across from a beautiful Georgian house, both recently built, was confounding everyone until we noticed, and then directed the client's gaze toward, the perfect deep green on the nearby dumpster. It helped that the sample was 20 feet (6 meters) long. Observing a model in Phillip Johnsond visual prec appropriated classic New England Barn Red and Asphalted Black for his Da Monsta gallery. Joe DyUrso found a Gainsburger when other reds fell short. Ross Bleckner unearthed a coffee bean to tint the perfect floor. Bill Liberman couldnoss from a beautiful Georgian house, both recently built's Contemporary Wing.

We have also learned to pay attention to admittedly strange and oblique direction. Peter Eisenman once described the palette he wanted for his buildings with whooshing sounds of different pitches. At that moment, in front of his model of rhythmically undulating structures, his noises made some sense.

One question often hanging in the air is, ne question often hanging in the air is adm, ne question often hanging in the air is admittedly str, ne question often hanging in the air is ads on accurately gauged levels and flows of light to calculate values. It is only after we determine lights and darks that each value can logically invite its appropriate hue. And even though we believe there are no "bad" colors, and clients are entitled to have the shades they love, personal color preferences can themselves be obstacles to a successful palette. We often urge all parties to put aside their preconceptions and allow the spaces to speak for themselves. Deeper colors might cause rooms without much natural light to glow, aligning with their dim illumination, whereas whites, most people's first thought for adding light, would leave them looking gloomy and unpainted.

Is it easier for clients and designers to find common ground by staying in the familiar realm of classical proportion and ornamentation to which this book is devoted? Precedents of classical forms can provide helpful arenas of shared understanding, and sometimes they do, but they may also distract from color's fine-tuning role, in adjusting interacting elements toward their intended balance. While classical disciplines provide proven guidelines for siting, hierarchies, and illumination, they don't elaborate on the details of the so-called skin on all these structures. Since our job is the skin, we believe the effort it takes for coloring, and thus shaping the shapes through color, depends not on style but on subtleties of color and finishes.

There is also a popular notion that new materials and methods of building are a richer source of inspiration than historical ones. We should applaud any sources captured by designers to fuel unique expressions, but we should also remember that even tiny increments of visual harmony, supplied by our living spaces, may elevate the everyday life of one person or an entire community. Colors on the inside belong to the inhabitants: on the outside, to the neighborhood. We believe you should consider both.

"Magic happens when craftsmen are allowed to employ their skills. A poetic resonance accumulates on the surface only when all the underlying, invisible layers of plaster, primers and paints are viewed as important as the topcoat." – Donald Kaufman

The formal rigor of classical styles has made working with them a treat, but the wide range of other architectural vocabularies on which we've been privileged to collaborate has driven home the lesson that aesthetic balance does not depend on any one particular precedent. Classical architecture has been effectively expressed in vastly divergent palettes. Nor does aesthetic harmony sink or swim on trends. Color palettes in built structures are ineliminable, and a painted room's character may come, in large part, from an inspired color scheme. The interaction between light and pigment, regardless of the hues being expressed, bring us the energy of light, a radiant flux, and condition the ultimate contribution of the space to our wellbeing.

Taffy and I see our job as formulating pigment mixtures, those 6-millimeter (0.2-inch) skeins of oil or acrylic, to create a poetic balance between the forms they cover and the light they absorb and reflect.

We try to remember to work with humor, simplicity, and careful listening. We were once asked to find a new color for Candlestick Park, the sports stadium in San Francisco. The Parks Department hired us after both the Giants and the 49ers had objected to using red, orange, yellow, blue, and purple. Taffy and I glanced at each other, pretended to think, and then suggested green. All were delighted. ❧

Use only white un-tinted primer unless otherwise specified. Like transparent watercolor, coatings create luminosity by allowing light to filter through the paint film and be reflected by the white substrate.

Donald Kaufman Color

The collaborative relationship between architect, decorator, and landscape designer is especially important in a tropical environment, where the line between inside and outside living sometimes become blurred.
Smith Architectural Group

A Builder's Perspective

John Rogers

My experience in building high quality homes has taught me that each project must be viewed with the same amount of importance. I understand the value of trust that clients place in my hands - and in the hands of their design team - and it is fair to say that we all strive for a successful outcome. It also goes without saying that a great deal of time and effort is invested into each and every project. So why is it that some projects are more successful than others?

More than often the difference in the final outcome is not due to a lack of experience or a lack of funding, but rather a lack of cohesion, decision making - and most importantly – collaboration, between the members of the design team. We, as the builders, are judged not only on the basis of uncompromising workmanship and service, but also the quality of the total experience for all parties involved. As such, collaboration is a fundamental component within our company and our profession. Without it the goal of delivering a successful project with a positive experience becomes much more challenging.

Collaboration is a term often used, but an act seldom performed. Nowadays it is constantly offered in sales and marketing materials as a key tenet for a company, or mentioned as a catch phrase in presentations. Yet, true collaborative relationships are in reality very rare, as sharing does not often come naturally

to many designers. No one designer – architect or decorator - can control all of a project's components and succeed. Indeed, most architects, interior designers and decorators, landscape architects, engineers, and consultants are focused on achieving their own individual objectives. True collaboration requires the sharing of knowledge and information by all of these parties, developing consensus through communication and working together to achieve the common goal of surpassing the expectations of the client, and delivering them the home of their dreams. In many instances, builders are not involved in the initial decision making or the design development phase of projects and are left to interpret, implement and coordinate decisions that were made without their input. The client typically engages the architect first, who then develops the project program in conjunction with the engineering and design consultants to represent the client's desires. In delivering a successful project, it is vital that the architect assume the leadership role and lead the communication as well as engaging the builder at these early stages. This communication—both early on in the design phase, and later during construction—enables efficiencies, as both parties have a different perspective and wealth of expertise to offer. The architect works to communicate the vision of the project by preparing construction documentation and project specifications that allow the builder to clearly interpret and implement the

Architect's intent through construction. The builder communicates to the architect the means and methods of achieving the end goal by constructing what is envisioned, as it relates to cost and the most feasible means of achieving this vision. A successful dialogue between the two parties can often result in a design component being modified to provide a better overall solution, or to save on the cost.

Ideally communication, coordination and collaboration should start early on in the design process - certainly prior to shovels in the ground - as once construction commences many changes can result in higher costs, coordination issues, a longer schedule, and a comprised design that negatively effects the quality of the home. The sooner that all parties are involved and on the same page, the better, and the less likely unnecessary changes will occur during construction.

Once construction commences, the builder then assumes the leadership role in order to implement the design teams vision and continue communication with the client, architect and other design professionals. Too often these other design professionals operate in a fragmented manner, with little communication between themselves and the architect, and even less or no communication with the builder – that is, until they propose a change to the design. In the typical design-bid-build process, the architect rarely has the time to solve all of the construction issues that may arise with the design at that stage of development. Likewise, most builders involved in a process such as this do not have the time to focus on resolving issues, therefore missing scope

and additional cost out of their bids. The architect and the builder have different goals in this scenario; one is focused on aesthetics and functionality, the other focused on cost, constructability and schedule. This is where inefficiencies, distrust, additional costs and further miscommunication can leave the client with an unpleasant experience throughout the process and potentially an unfavorable end result.

So, how do we utilize collaboration to improve the relationships as well as the performance of the design team and the builder? And, more importantly, how can collaboration benefit the home owner? The best homes are realized with a continued dialogue between the architect, home owner, consultants and builder. So, with that in mind:

The basis for success and a true collaboration is started when the Architect assembles a design team where there is a diversity of knowledge and experience that complements their own. It is important to create a team environment where openness is welcomed in order to produce an integrated and collaborative outcome.

An early involvement of the entire team (Architect, Decorator, Consultants and Builder) lends itself to a better understanding and appreciation of each other's role in the project. Roles are clearly defined with clear communication of the goals and desired outcome. Creating an environment of respect and candid communication also develops the relationship and closeness between parties.

Utilizing the concept of vernacular progression, Anglo, French, and Spanish architectural elements combine to create a house that appears to have grown and evolved over time.
Ken Tate Architect

This loggia, overlooking the lush gardens and swimming pool, is divided into different areas that allow for outside dining and entertaining.
Smith Architectural Group

There has to be an acceptance that all parties are focused on the same goal - which is to deliver a successful project on time, on budget, while also exceeding the client's expectations. This approach leads to a familiarity with each other that can only benefit the project, as well as future projects down the road.

When challenges arise, there is no finger pointing. Instead, everyone lends their diverse knowledge and expertise to create solutions and maintain momentum. Involving craftsmen and artisans early in the process is also a key move, as they can offer unique perspectives that will significantly contribute towards a more beautiful and more efficient end result.

In this specialized segment of the industry, a builder's reputation is a critical factor. It is important for builders to always strive to cultivate working relationships with design consultants, engineers, and craftsmen. Preparation, communication and implementation is a good mantra – as clients, design professionals and builders alike, cannot afford the cost and exhaustion of poor coordination. As a builder of the highest quality, my aim has always been to exceed the client's expectations and provide them with a level of service that reflects the collaborative approach as much as possible. The first rule is to create an environment where input can be shared freely, with a level of candor, while maintaining a friendly and enjoyable working atmosphere. This enables all parties to move forward and work toward solutions without the feeling that an individual team member may have an agenda that is separate from the common goal. An open book approach is the most effective, where the home owner is involved throughout the process as much or as little as they desire to be. Working together with the design team, the client is given a home that is not only an architectural show piece, but filled with the warmth a home owner expects when they move in. By faithfully serving clients through a truly collaborative effort, builders will not only build homes, but will build relationships with all parties involved which will create additional opportunities in the future – as partnerships continue long after the client receives the keys to their new home. ✵

ABOVE:
A design rendering for a Anglo-Caribbean style house in Florida. The rear façade, dominated by its Jeffersonian double portico, provides sweeping views of the Atlantic and continues the grand tradition of classical architecture in the Palm Beach area.

Magnolia and the repetition of rounded boxwoods create a subtle boarder around an entrance court.
Doyle Herman Design Associates

The Merger of Living and Built

James Doyle and Kathryn Herman

Collaborations come in many guises and as business partners we embraced ours over 15 years ago. This was based on a symbiotic relationship complimenting each other's strengths and weaknesses and with mutual interests in associated arts such as horticulture, architecture, art history, and landscape history. We shared the same romantic notions of building beautiful landscapes and building a business that would evolve with us. Years later, our goals remain shared as we strive to create extraordinary design by integrating artistic expression within the contextual perspective of the presented architecture.

Client relationships are always at the forefront of our projects. They lead us with their requests, both specific and non-specific, and we play the roles of educator and editor. As well, we look to deliver on clientuests, both specific and non would evolve with us. Years larate a harmonizing result between architecture and its surrounding landscape. Our clients also lead us to their chosen team of architects and interior designers and here the collaboration becomes a vital process. Not only does it need to happen between all interested parties, for us, it must occur with nature. Plant material—one of our principal materials—can take years to develop and can thrive or fail based on nature educator and editor. As well, we look to deliver on clientuests, both specideveloping landscape. We ask clients to remember that, sometimes, our completed work is in its initial stage and will only increase in enjoyment as it develops from year to year.

We work closely with nurserymen, who have had the foresight to grow plant material for years that we then use as mature specimens. Sometimes this is a true act of faith by the nurserymen, but we have also developed relationships where plant material is grown for our specific use. Our projects lead us to collaborate with other professionals such as ecologists, structural and civil engineers, surveyors, and contractors and without these relationships our projects fail.

A truly successful project is one where there is great architecture, beautiful interiors, and an enchanting landscape. We liken this to a stool—without those three legs, it falls flat.

Gardens are an expression of personal taste just as the way in which interior rooms are furnished and decorated. Yet gardens are more than an exercise in exterior decoration because they involve a living environment. We, as designers, are involved with the earth itself. We are inspired by landscapes and architecture of the past but interpret these for the more modern lifestyles of our clients. Our designs are the link between the interior and the exterior and we do this with terraces, courtyards, and axial views to termination points such as water features, fire features, and garden ornamentation. We satisfy our collaborators, (clients, architects, and decorators) with these physical and visual links. We strive to enhance the architecture of the home, perhaps by bringing to prominence a portico, or we take inspiration from an arcade with its arches and columns and we recreate this effect in the landscape by manipulating our plant material. The interior décor can influence our choice of colors in herbaceous borders or dictate a more relaxed or strict landscape. They can also inform our choices for the fabric on our selected outdoor furnishings. In residential design, the architect, landscape designer, and interior decorator partner to develop a common vision.

The images accompanying this text exemplify a wonderful collaboration that portrayed trust and faith and a running dialog with all involved. Our firm came recommended to the clients by the architects and so began a design project that enriched all of our experiences.

On another project of ours that became a Palladio Award winner for the landscape, a new home was built, but the landscape came with existing majestic trees that included a chestnut, weeping beech, and magnolia. These provided a foundation that acted as the grounding element to the new house. Every aspect of the landscape was reimagined but with deference to these trees. The clients asked for collaboration with the architectural firm to ensure a fitting landscape. The overall vision for our design was derived from the placement and orientation of the house and the preservation of these sacred icons.

Sometimes the best landscape elements are those that play a lesser role to the architecture and this is a philosophy that we carry throughout all our projects.

It may be a small plat of pachysandra, with sole rounded boxwoods that plays off the main block of the house. It may be the trees that we add to ground the house with their vertical presence. Details such as inlays of bluestone in a parking courtyard can further enhance the core of the building.

We sometimes begin our axial gestures at the front of the home and carry them through the house where they terminate further beyond in the garden. These terminal points offer another opportunity to collaborate with artists and their artwork, so commissioning and site placement is an important part of our process. For example, as shown here, a striking modern sculpture of polished stainless steel by David Harber infused the traditional design with a sense of modernity.

On past projects, we have looked to repurpose remnants that existed on a site we were going to completely redesign. For example, large slabs of stone were saved from the previous house and reused as treads in the main lawn staircase, which then traversed from the rear terrace down toward a pool. This staircase had deep plantings of billowing boxwoods either side that narrowed as they approached the pool. This purposeful forced perspective added a sense of depth to the property. There is also a great sense of satisfaction in honoring the past life of a property.

Throughout all of our projects, we have seen the benefit of collaboration play out. Everyone involved brings something different to the table. The depth of skills, expertise, and knowledge is an incredibly valuable resource—one only needs to have an open mind and listen. ❧

A modern sculpture of polished stainless steel by David Harber terminates the long axial view from the house, through the gardens, to the swimming pool.
Doyle Herman Design Associates

HARMONY FARM: The architecture and the gardens are successfully woven together, by constructing a series of stone retaining walls that shape the natural sloping land into flat usable garden parterres, each accessed and overlooked from a different room in the house.
Hamady Architects with Doyle Herman Design Associates

A Visit to the Mount

Kahlil Hamady

The practice of architecture requires a profound understanding of the multidisciplines necessary for the recreation of space and the relationships between them. The history of classical and traditional architecture offers rich examples by those who have practiced with such conscious awareness. Just as John Singer Sargent delights the visitors of The Museum of Fine Arts in Boston with his murals at the dome representing the figure of Architecture embracing and protecting Painting and Sculpture, Renaissance Architecture could not flourish without the coexistence of, and the symphonic interplays among, the subjects of architecture, painting, sculpture, landscape, furniture design, music, mythology, and literature. Michelangelo, Bernini and Da Vinci, to name only a few, crossed freely the boundaries between those fields, drawing lessons from one and applying them to the other. Classical culture did not merely consider such attempts as part of a unique manner of composition but rather as a complete state of being, feeling, and thinking of the world and the way to engage it.

In the first chapter of his first book *De Architectura*, the Roman architect Vitruvius describes the 12 fields of studies necessary for the education and practice of the architect: astronomy, writing, drafting, geometry, optics, arithmetic, history, philosophy, physics, music, law, and medicine. And while it may appear curious for a modern mind to consider Alberti optics, arithmetic, history, philosophy, and architecture in one chapter in his architectural treatise, *De Re Aedificatoria*, the Classical mind inherently acknowledged the interrelationship between subjects bound by the presence of a universal knowledge and the timeless principles and patterns that permeated these fields. Within this mental construct, time and space appear more cohesive.

Today, this spherical awareness seems to have been forgotten and replaced with a different state. The segregation of those disciplines as separate and unrelated entities is due to multiple reasons: the emphasis on scientific and educational specializations; empirical, focused, and reductionist measurements of one's wellbeing, (physical or economical, individual or collective); the fractional dissection of time; the weakening of the education, practice, and role of the architect; the devaluation of the merit of the subject and the collective focus on rapid progress in technology. The cumulative result of such conditions is the fragmentation of spatial experiences and its resulting interruption in the flow of mental understanding of space as a comprehensive whole. Human capacity to understand, experience and recreate coherent and cohesive spatial conditions, even by those who practice in those related fields, has become greatly impaired.

History, however, embodies wisdom as she reminds us of the enduring and important knowledge that transcends time and provides a record for evolving cultures to examine their present and past as a means to correct their paths. As we recall the interests and contributions of Thomas Jefferson in various disciplines including architecture, we reach out to our recent history, to the literary and architectural works of Edith Wharton and the representation of the complete awareness of the intertwined nature of those subjects.

Prior to creating her sanctum at the Mount, Wharton first examined with architect Ogden Codman, Jr. in their book, *The Decoration of Houses*, published in 1897, the subject of architecture and interior design. Her contribution to an intellectual record of awareness preceded her act of visual creation in 1902. History reveals that the composition of enduring space requires purposeful intentions described through a visual or literary narrative. Memorable houses, temples and cities are imagined as meaningful thoughts, founded on principles and values, narrated first in words and drawings and immortalized in stone and wood. The idea of Rome is recalled through her legends of Aeneas and Romulus and Remus, as recorded by Virgil for the Emperor Augustus and experienced as a state of interrelated indoor and outdoor spaces under the cycles of the days, the seasons, and the years. The experiences of those external states are first composed through an inner narrative, be it mythical, poetic, literary, or artistic.

For Wharton, she established through her first book the literary foundation that propelled her onto the national stage. As she established an intellectual authority, which stated the rational relationships between the subjects of architecture and interior design and the order and principles that governed both, she ventured into a visual creation that involved architecture, interiors, gardens, and natural landscape. The significance of the intertwining of those subjects at the Mount is reminiscent of the way the Ancients thought of the purposeful composition of space. The most meaningful and profound aspect in her accomplished works lies in the implied literary composition woven through those subjects as she created a complete visual, emotional, and mental experience of a place.

Wharton's success is based on a keen interest in and understanding of the human condition, which helped her create timeless literary and visual compositions that are intuitively understood. As in the order in which humans are disposed to follow a story or read a book, eat a meal or watch a play, listen to a musical composition or simply follow the sun, there is a beginning and a procession both of linear and concurrent cues and events. At the Mount, while Wharton's and composition begins at the gatehouse, its prelude unfolds as the visitor travels the gentle hills of the Berkshires in western Massachusetts.

Wharton sought refuge in nature, away from the distorting material world, which engulfed Newport in the late 19th century. As in those days, one still feels the escape from the populated centers, leaving the energies of the city to draw inspiration from nature. Once past the boundary of the public road and the threshold of the gatehouse, one sweeps into the sanctuary of an enchanted forest, abandoning oneself

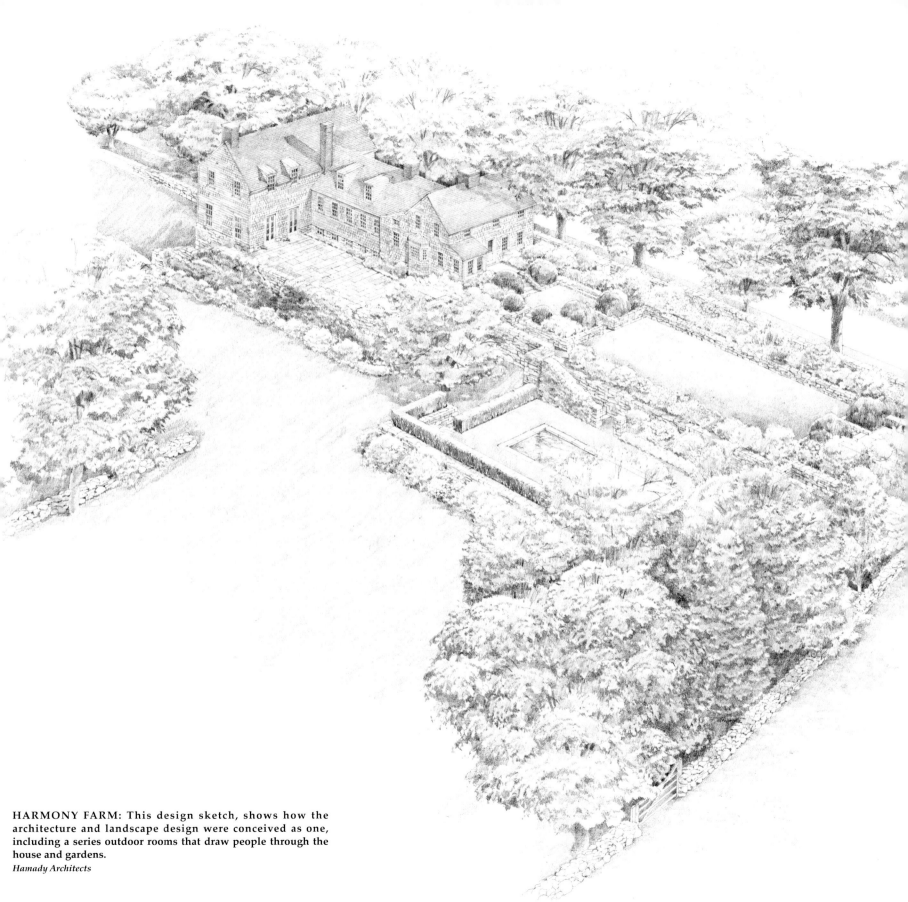

HARMONY FARM: This design sketch, shows how the architecture and landscape design were conceived as one, including a series outdoor rooms that draw people through the house and gardens.
Hamady Architects

to the uncertainties of the natural environment, through a softly curving drive, the only sign of civility. Past a creek, the visitor captures a glimpse of a place as one continues a seemingly literary and lyrical procession.

Approaching the house from the northern and dark side, two piers framing the forecourt and the central part of the house remind the visitor, through a choreographed composition, as to who is fit to be allowed into the inner sanctuary. Entering the space, the visitor senses that the house has been embedded in the rocky land, and the architecture, through the walls of the courtyard, extends into the landscape harboring and embracing the newly arrived traveler. As it is unfamiliar to expect such abrupt architectural verticality in a New England forest, the imagery of a temple cannot be missed, through which one enters from the underworld, a mythical place from which humans emerged through a vertical procession to the realm above. Ascension is written all over the façade through its proportions and composition. The space immediately evokes the rituals of the Eleusinian mysteries and the imageries of Persephone, reenacting her cyclical and seasonal birth.

The visitor enters the house through a dark vaulted foyer, its walls expressed in plastered Tufa, completing the illusion of a grotto and the extension of the landscape into the interior spaces. There, Wharton made her guests wait on a stone bench, until they were deemed fit to pass through and depart from this subterranean space. Through this passage at the end of the foyer, the visitor proceeds to a naturally lit vertical space occupied by a

stairwell emerging fluidly to the second floor above, a place representing the earthly state within the classical tripartite composition of space. Following a carefully timed moment of pause from the ascension, a horizontal gallery draws the visitor to a regal procession to admire evocative artifacts of travelled places. The lofty space provides the guest a moment to catch a breath and a glimpse of the forecourt from which one has just emerged. To the other side, one's entry is celebrated through an arched passage leading to the living room, drawing the visitor's eye upward to its elaborately adorned ceiling. The crescendo of this carefully choreographed procession is the arrival to the south-facing terrace, with its sweeping views of the formal gardens in the foreground and the natural landscape beyond. Here is the moment of emergence, of rebirth, of renewal.

The axial composition of the house extends into the landscape. For Wharton, the garden is the realm between the house and the natural world, drawing its raw materials from one and its composition from the other. While their ingredients may differ, gardens remain as exterior spaces and rooms that are governed by similar principles relevant to architecture and interior spaces, the whole narrated by a master plan encompassing all of them. The order of the procession through the indoor and outdoor spaces is a classic form, which never fails to delight a being, regardless of time, place or culture. While the siting of the Mount is according to Vitruvius and the procession through the house is suggestive of the Platonic myth of light. The vertical ascension evokes a recurring theme in western mythology and classical space composition. This theme is exemplified in the aforementioned account of the cyclical rebirth of Persephone or the autochthonous birth of Erichthonius, ascending as Athena received the king of Athens from Gaia. In this literary and visual composition, Wharton used all subjects—nature, landscape, garden design, architecture and interior design—to provide a complete experience through which she found inspiration in a visual reenactment of a myth timelessly relevant.

A contemporary example that follows the model of the Mount lies at one of my recently completed projects—Harmony Farm in Greenwich, Connecticut. Situated at the edge of an old trail in South Connecticut, the original 18th-century farmhouse is a remnant of the simple New England vernacular architecture of the time. Collaborating with Doyle Herman Design Associates, from the onset through the development of a master plan, the design of the indoor and the outdoor spaces were weaved through complete and linked processions that returned to the preserved 18th-century farmhouse a useful and delightful presence. The sequential arrangement of those spaces was carefully examined, beginning with the entry to the property proceeding through the forecourt to the house and into the terraces, the gardens, and landscape beyond. Consideration of the architecture, the interiors, and the gardens could not be separated without the loss of the intended experience. The house without its gardens would appear isolated. The gardens without the house would loose their purpose. The interiors would seem meaningless without the two. Using judiciously the universal principles of composition including order, symmetry, eurhythmy, arrangement, appropriateness, and economy, both house and gardens created an intimate corner of the universe from which one feels centered and safe to imagine the world beyond.

During her years at the Mount, Wharton wrote some of her most significant work, *The House of Mirth* and *Italian Gardens and Their Villas*. During the course of her life, she published 40 books, was nominated for Nobel prizes, won the first female Pulitzer award in Literature and received an honorary degree from Yale University in 1923. More importantly, thanks to its preservation, we inherited at the Mount a time-tested model of composition for designers, patrons, and enthusiasts to examine and follow in the creation of our own comprehensive spaces. ✤

PAGE 72:
HARMONY FARM: By preserving the modest scale and simple geometry of the original house, the new architecture maintained a restrained and measured articulation of space and detail. The entrance parterre is framed and enclosed by a low masonry wall, and a structured, yet pared down, aerial hedge.
Hamady Architects with Doyle Herman Design Associates

OPPOSITE:
HARMONY FARM: From the onset of the project, architect Kahlil Hamady focused on the concurrent study of the architecture, its interiors and the surrounding landscape as interrelated subjects. Here is a view from inside the house, overlooking the terraced formal gardens and bucolic landscape beyond.
Hamady Architects with Doyle Herman Design Associates

Francis Terry with plasterers from Locker and Riley making clay models of the Lafranchini stucco work at Castletown, County Kildare, Ireland.

Quinlan & Francis Terry Architects

Fortune Favors the Friendly

Francis Terry

On occasion, I meet architects who think that they are or, more often, should be 'in charge' of every aspect of their buildings. These people are either very naive or deluded. They hark back to a golden age when architects were taken seriously like doctors or lawyers and paid a proper fee. They fail to grasp the essence of architecture and an easier life. The trick is to collaborate—do your bit well and don't overstretch yourself. Let others do the parts you struggle with, freeing you up to do the design without worrying about things that may obstruct sound architectural judgment.

The Royal Institute of British Architects (RIBA) and the architectural press often bemoan the inevitable erosion of the architect's role, as project managers, planning consultants, and contractors eliminate their traditional duties. This is part of a broader trend towards specialization. Eighteenth-century philosopher and economist Adam Smith's theory for the division of labor has at last alighted on architecture and the profession, like legendary King Canute, attempts to hold back the inevitable tide. Unlike many of my peers, I welcome this situation. I did not come into architecture to administer contracts, fill out planning forms or take responsibility for damp proofing, all of which I have only a superficial knowledge at best. I came into architecture to design buildings and if someone wants to take the more mundane yet essential supporting jobs away from me, I say, "Bring it on!"

Collaboration comes in many forms: collaboration with clients, fellow professionals, builders, craftsmen, and work colleagues.

When you think of really great structures like the pyramids, the Pantheon or Versailles, the architect's name almost seems irrelevant pitched against the titanic will of their patron. And rightly the pharaohs, Emperor Hadrian and Louis XIV are seen as the driving force behind their most celebrated works of architecture. Seeing London's St Paul's cathedral as being designed by Sir Christopher Wren is really not the whole story. The idea for a classical domed cathedral, which had no precedent in English architecture, must have been the brainchild of King Charles II who had seen similar buildings while exiled in France. Likewise, the architectural detailing was probably designed by master masons with Wren's consent. Precious few construction drawings were done of the cathedral and very few by Wren's hand. For example, the Corinthian capitals of the cathedral's lower order are among the most beautiful by any standard, owing more to the work of sculptors in the tradition of Grindling Gibbons than Wren, who was a mathematician and astronomer by training with little practical experience of sculpture or architectural ornament.

This is certainly my experience of clients. They are, for better or worse, the driving force behind everything about a project. I have had clients who have educated me and changed the way I design through their perfectionism and eye for detail. At other times a client will not listen and I end up designing something which I knew, could be better, but the happiness of the client is the goal of every project.

A successful project relies on a group of designers working collaboratively to ensure the best result. At the time of writing, I am working on a house where we have a very cohesive professional team. I sit around the table with the garden designer and interior designer and between us we refine the scheme and, in so doing, improve it from all points of view. A certain degree of detachment by everyone is necessary so that each professional can work to the best of their ability. A well-run contract is like being part of an orchestra; everyone does their part well leaving space for others to perform their role. I had a client recently who wanted a classical exterior and a modern interior. For this I paired up with a contemporary designer, we established the extent of each other's remit and it all worked very well. The alternative would be for me to force the client to have a classical interior against their wishes or try to design modern-style interiors myself. Neither situation would have ended well.

Collaboration with builders is essential for architects. If the architect falls into the trap of feeling that he must control everything the builder does, he will very soon be in deep water. The way an architect realizes a good building is to only insist on what is important to him and allow the builder to do his part, unhindered by the architect's half baked ideas. An increasing amount of building contracts allow the builders to design and take responsibility for elements of work. This way of working is resented by many architects as they view it as yet another nail in the coffin of their hallowed profession.

Take the issue of damp proofing, a remit increasingly given over to builders. Traditionally, architects would draw out damp proof courses including axonometric sketches of how the various sheets of material meet on awkward junctions. The draftsman detailing these elements had probably never touched a damp-proof membrane and so would know next to nothing about the practicalities of the details he was drawing. In this situation, the builder has no incentive to make sure it works. His attitude will be, "Mr. Architect has detailed this, I know it's not going to work but what do I care, he is the person to blame, not me." A better situation is for the builder to take responsibility for damp-proofing design and installation. This will motivate him to do the best job he could with the materials of his choice. The architect would need to know the visual impact of the damp proofing and that it works, but nothing more.

As with a builder, to have a successful collaboration with a craftsman you need to know what to draw and, equally important, what not to draw. For example, when working on full-size drawings of classical ornament, we often adapt our details to suit the material in which the object is to be made. For example, if it is to be cast, we think how the mold can be removed and, if carved, we think about how the mason will be able to get his chisel in for undercutting. I have recently discovered that this is not a good way of working, and again collaboration holds the key. It is much better to design exactly the form you want, meet with the craftsman and discuss how this can be achieved. If your detail is impossible to make, compromise then and not beforehand. Conversely, you will find that some part you thought was very hard to make is in fact very easy.

A detail of the Ionic capital at Hanover Lodge in Regents Park, London, inspired by the Erechtheion in Athens (421-405 BC). The neck of column is decorated with a stylized anthemion, which differentiates it from all other Greek capitals.
Quinlan & Francis Terry Architects

The entrance façade of Hanover Lodge is dominated by a full-height portico that recalls the neoclassical architecture of Karl Friedrich Schinkel in Berlin.
Quinlan & Francis Terry Architects

A good collaboration with a craftsman is one of the great pleasures of architecture. Recently, I designed a ceiling for a client in Ireland who was keen to have a Rococo design in the style of the Lafranchini brothers, who worked in Ireland during the 18th century. In order to do this, I went with the modelers to see some Lafranchini work in the flesh. We got permission to bring tools and clay into a Lafranchini house to copy the work there. I spent some time modeling with the craftsmen, which in turn gave me greater insight into the Lafranchini brothers' work and the issues to look out for when inspecting the new ceiling. Needless to say this was a very enjoyable experience and made a huge difference to the quality of the final work.

Work colleagues have a lot to contribute to the design process. Some architects feel the need to design in isolation. They shut the door and draw. The problem with this way of working is that very quickly you will not be able to see the wood for the trees. You will end up pleasing yourself but not actually doing a good piece of architecture. Good design needs to have a rational answer to all criticism. It should take on ideas from anyone, particularly people who are not part of the profession as their view is often better than those directly involved. This is very much my approach when I design. I welcome people coming in and passing comment. Some of these views are worth listening to others not, but I value the interaction and having my preconceptions challenged.

When I was growing up, I was torn between wanting to be an artist and an architect, a common dilemma, which has faced many artistic students. Having completed my architectural qualifications and worked for some time in offices I decided to dedicate myself completely to painting. After three years, I gave up and returned to architecture, the reason for this really goes to the heart of the nature of collaboration. Before this painting episode I would see people working in supermarkets and in my rather patronizing way, I would feel sorry for them. I felt that if only they could be freed from the humdrum reality of paying the rent they could dedicate themselves to some artistic enterprise of their own. Perhaps writing a novel or whatever they pleased. As I began to find the life of an artist increasingly lonely I would see the same people and actually feel quite jealous. They had a purpose, they were necessary and while they did their jobs they could happily have a joke with their peers or share their stories. They were embodied in life in a way that a lone struggling artist can only dream. I wanted this connection with life, I am sure the Renaissance artist working on his frescos would have been involved in a similar social endeavor, but the modern artist is a very isolated figure. I missed the office banter, the discussions with clients and builders. I missed having deadlines and feeling part of something bigger. In short, I missed the collaboration on a work of art, which was too big for me to create by myself.

Painting is of course one of the highest and most intense art forms, but it is small and personal, great as Vermeer undoubtedly is, his entire surviving works could easily fit in a typical self storage unit. Architecture, on the other hand, paints on a far broader canvas, which requires the collaboration of many differently skilled people in its execution and this is, in essence, the joy of architecture. ❧

Fully versed in historic precedent, and working from design sketches and charcoal renderings, artisans use time honored techniques to sculpt and cast some of the finest plaster ornamentation available.
Foster Reeve & Associates

The Plaster Artisan

Foster Reeve

Thankfully for the plaster artisan, there is a movement on many premier projects toward a more effective collaboration between architecture and interior design. This union is central to fully utilizing the advantages of plasterwork. The myriad options for using plaster—from the highly ornamental to the more modern detailing, as well as all of the beautiful integral colored castings and finishes—are not often fully addressed in the construction phase of a project. However, this is precisely where they need to be developed, designed, budgeted, and approved. But doesn't this type of arrangement run against the economic model of the strategically managed project? Why should we concern ourselves with collaboration with any artisan?

What defines a good artisan is their dedication to excellence in the craft. They study, practice, and research the intricacies of the work and its application. They embrace new practices and set them upon the stable history of the craft. A good artisan stands on the shoulders of the past as they seek to develop better methods and products for the new work of today. In plasterwork, collaboration with the artisan sets the stage for the development of high quality, healthful, enduring, and beautiful interior spaces that take the architect and designer's vision into reality.

Plaster is often not fully understood by the design and building communities. It is an extremely versatile product whose use is limited only by the imagination of the designer. Plaster is comprised of essentially calcium, the fifth most abundant element in the crust of the earth, in seawater, and in the human body. It is green in that it produces a naturally antimicrobial surface, and contains no harmful chemicals that will contaminate the interior environment. It is fireproof. It is stable, meaning no cracking or movement over time that will necessitate inconvenient and costly touch-ups and repairs. It has the rare quality of being able to be easily formed into many shapes, using many methods both ancient and modern. Because it is often poorly understood, particularly in the U.S., it is frequently overlooked by the design and building communities. However, these are precisely the reasons that collaboration with the plaster artisan, at the earliest stages of the design process, are often a major benefit to any significant project. Let me share with you some of my experiences.

Regarding economy, I recall a project that involved 18 groin vaults and arches forming the ceiling of three sides of an enclosed cloister. The contractor was pursuing pricing to have these executed in traditional three-coat plaster over wire and framing, with an alternate for sectioned drywall and framing. I had been invited by the owner's representative to review the plaster program for potential cost savings and for quality assurance. When I saw the plans for this area, I suggested a precast GFRG (glass fiber reinforced gypsum) paneled system. This suggestion saved the owner a significant sum, and produced much finer detailing in the paneled arches than would have been attainable in either of the other systems. Had the owner's rep not had the foresight to invite us in for an early review of the project, much time would have been wasted pursuing the wrong specification, and perhaps even executing it. Thus, collaboration is essential from the early stages of the design, development and budgeting in order to determine if and how plaster could be appropriate.

Along the same lines, I recently created a complex curved umbrella vault—based upon a similar one in historic Kronborg Castle in Denmark (better known as *Elsinore* in William Shakespeare's *Hamlet*). The original vault would have been hand-built by the plaster artisan using templates and screeds— which is exactly how many builders might still consider building it nowadays. However, the modern architect and builder should be aware that this (and other similar radial and groin vault ceilings) can be constructed much more economically in a precast gypsum system, requiring no framing—but simply being hung from existing rafters or joists. These design opportunities in combination with construction considerations make collaborating with the plaster artisan early in a project a potentially rewarding prospect in the development of the aesthetics, and in the control of the budget.

No more so, was this approach utilized than when working on Ravenwood[1] in Pennsylvania. Here, much of the architecture was based upon historic an English Georgian precedent. In recreating the look and feel of the decorative plaster ceilings, we were challenged to develop a module that could be rotated and adjusted, and with just enough hand-applied pieces, to give it the unique, handmade asymmetry of each *rinceaux* spiral. This was only possible because the architect Richard Cameron, assigned us the task of developing this design, along with presenting the budget, and fought to have it approved by the owner. I must admit that the contractor I-Grace and, in particular, their representative on the project Tony Hume, were very supportive of this process with a keen awareness that to get something special everyone needed to be pulling in the same direction.

Working on an Art Deco-inspired design by Richard Landry in Los Angeles; we were tasked with developing the construction in plaster of the entire interior surface of the principle rooms of a Beverly Hills residence. This design included scalloped walls sometimes on complex curved surfaces and natural finishes as well. Joan Benke was the interior designer driving this part of our work and overseeing the collaboration between all parties, including the visionary contractor John Finton. While Joan shepherded the process and ensured that deadlines and budgets were managed without sacrificing quality, many intricate design details were also hammered out by the entire teams close collaboration. With expertise in the design and finishing of their work, the plaster artisan brings insights and capabilities to the table,

1 For further detailed information on Ravenwood, I thoroughly recommend architect Richard Cameron's essay "Ravenwood, Newtown Square, Pennsylvaniana," in the first volume of this series. See Phillip James Dodd, *The Art of Classical Details: Theory, Design and Craftsmanship* (Images Publishing, 2013), pp. 140–143.

Custom crafted plaster fretwork and a floral centerpiece decorate the dining room ceiling at Ravenwood.
Foster Reeve & Associates

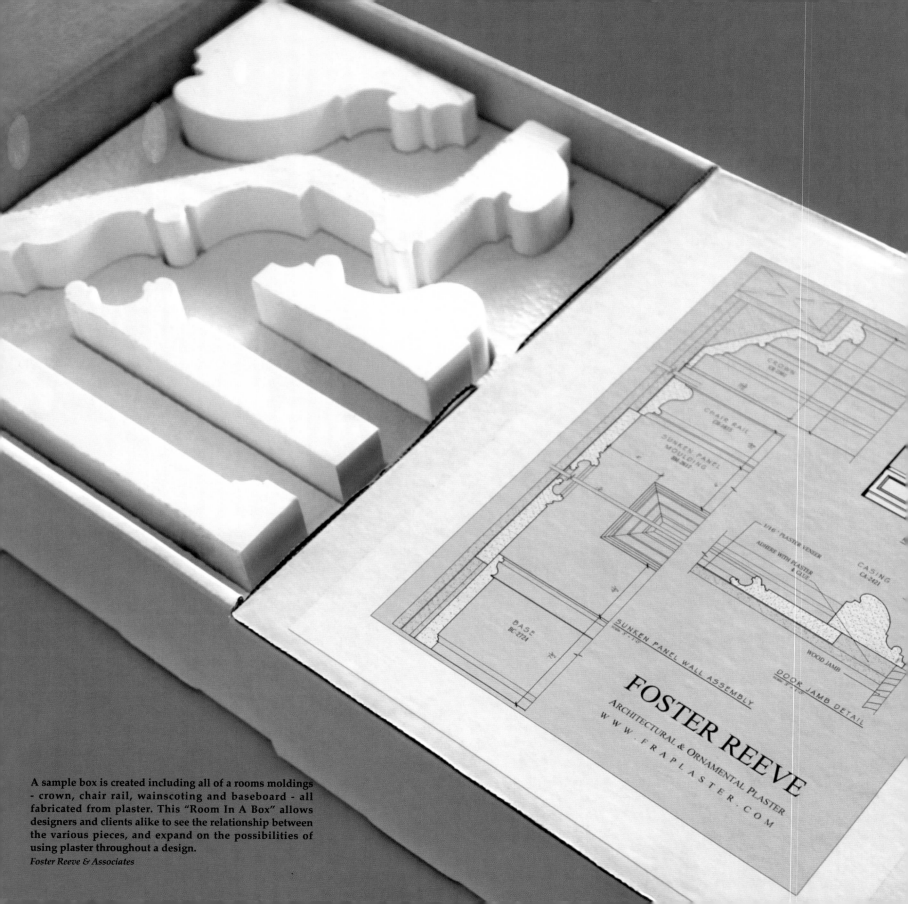

A sample box is created including all of a rooms moldings - crown, chair rail, wainscoting and baseboard - all fabricated from plaster. This "Room In A Box" allows designers and clients alike to see the relationship between the various pieces, and expand on the possibilities of using plaster throughout a design.

Foster Reeve & Associates

and designers and builders realize the full benefit of collaboration with a plaster artisan by engaging them early in the process.

Due in part to our long relationship, Rose Tarlow is one of my favorite designers. Her methods seem simple and direct. Rose will bring us to a project, outline her vision of the design, and then task us with copious sampling and mockups, providing options and ideas for development. No pushover on quality and very focused on her vision of how the elements of each artisans work fits into her overall design, Rose trusts that the process and the team she handpicks will provide the quality ingredients of a spectacular project. Rose successfully inspires and utilizes the creative genius of all the artisans on her projects.

Even in China we have found successful collaboration on a project with a visionary owner. Due to the high humidity in the region, the owner elected to have most of the interior trim and surfaces in plaster. Wanting a richly decorated neo-Classical home, the owner commissioned Richard Landry to design a spectacular residence and we were bought in to assist in developing the ornamentation for the plasterwork. Trust was very important to moving this collaboration forward so we were very generous with our knowledge going in, and this helped to propel a spirit of common purpose and excellence that assisted in bridging the cultural divide.

Collaboration in the world of building is fundamental to excellence. Design opportunities in combination with construction considerations make collaborating with the plaster artisan early in a project a potentially rewarding prospect in the development of the aesthetics, and in the control of the budget. Defining how that collaboration unfolds is predicated on the specific goals of the work to be done. When a beautiful interior is the mission, then it is paramount that someone—owner, architect, designer, or builder—has the knowledge and resources to pick the important artisans at an early stage to assist in developing the architects' and designers' vision, and help in developing the budget and schedule. The result is a cohesive team with a common goal and a commitment to providing the best work and, thus, the best value to the owner. ✤

ABOVE:
Craftsmen under-cutting the egg-and-dart molding on an ornate plaster crown, that includes intricate acanthus brackets, and rosettes set within the coffers.
Foster Reeve & Associates

Armed with a rich archive of samples, photographs, publications and catalogues, Nanz has created a line of door hardware which stretch from the historic to the avant-garde.
The Nanz Company

Manufactured to Please

Carl Sorenson

Not only do door handles combine functional aspects with issues of aesthetics in equal proportion, they are also the point at which the owner and his home come into contact with one another.

I grew up in a house in Ohio built in 1922 by a local architect of some reputation, Charles E Firestone. The home of stone and brick, with a two-story slate roof, employed cast bronze knobs with gothic tracery on 1.75-inch (4.5-centimeter) oak-paneled doors. While they were not my favorite knobs they were extremely well made and impressive with their accompanying rosettes, thumb turns and well-fashioned bit key locks. While I was entirely unaware, at the time, that they were a knob by the Yale Manufacturing Company and a fine example of the current 1920s technology, I did appreciate their quality.

The back of the house had plainer hardware, which I would later realize was the lesser of a two-tier hardware organizational system, the service hardware. The hardware in the house, along with the other aspects, was from a point in time where things were extremely well designed and well made. This generally held true throughout America up until WWII when manufacturing took a turn for the worse. Quality was sacrificed to accommodate the huge mass production required for the post-war construction boom. We were still in this dark period when I was graduating from college to enter the work force.

After school, I took several sales positions for large manufacturing companies. The first put me on the road pitching pipe tools to plumbing distributors and the second, heavy electrical equipment in New Jersey. However, I longed for what I hoped to be a more creative job, and to work in Manhattan where my friends all lived. One of those friends, a college pal named Steve Nanz was doing work for a builder who was restoring an apartment in the landmark Dakota. I visited him after work one evening (he had a shop on the third floor of a tenement building on the Bowery). On his workbench were some spring-loaded bronze cabinet latches, brass offset pivot hinges, and some interesting transom hinges. I was immediately attracted to the array of interesting metal forms and inquired about their origin. Steve explained that he reproduced classic hardware, which was no longer readily available. I was intrigued and after further questioning, I think we both felt there might be an opportunity to help one another. Steve was great at making things but far less interested in promoting himself or his work. We founded what was then Nanz Custom Hardware Inc., which was truly the first example of collaboration between the two partners themselves and their respective talents.

Nanz began by reproducing period hardware for Park Avenue and Upper East Side townhouses, designed by architects such as Rosario Candella, James Carpenter, and Mott Schmidt. While clients wanted to redo everything in their new home, they wanted to restore the hardware because, if for no other reason, it was original to the building. That's where Nanz would help. We would remove and organize the hardware and we would restore the hinges, repair the locks, and refinish the handles. One thing was true on every project—there were never enough handles to go around, and that's when we began manufacturing door hardware. It was not long before architects were asking us to design and fabricate custom "never seen before" handles.

Early in the company history, Jed Johnson and Alan Wanzenberg asked if we could make Rhullman-inspired handles for a French modern art and furniture collector. Alan handed me a Jacque Emil Rhullman monograph. I poured over the pages looking at what were mostly furniture designs with just a few metal details. I made some meticulous drawings of what I thought was an appropriate handle and had Steve fashion the lever in brass. As we had yet to understand casting methods of tool making or even basic machining techniques, Steve whittled the prototype from a brass bar using only the belt sander and a polishing wheel. It worked, however, and after a gentle critique the handle that was used on the project along with some custom drop pulls and thumb turns, was fashioned, approved, and purchased. We did and have done many similar projects for others which have included the influences of Carl Aubock, Pierre Charaux, Diego Giacometti, and Jean Despres to name a few.

Much of the work we do comes from our New York design studio. We have several experts who work in wood, wax, or metal to create new designs to our own specifications or to those of our clients. We often work with artists whose work we find interesting. By combining our expertise in hardware engineering and manufacturing methods with the artist's creative vision, we come up with some very imaginative solutions. When necessary, we can use modern scanning and rapid prototyping technology to create new designs. While our studio is often the 'Fertile Crescent' for our new ideas, it is at our 50,000-square-foot (4,645-square-meter) factory on Long Island that we manufacture our orders.

We have a deep bench of highly skilled workers who have been honing their skills for the majority of their careers. Some have been with us for over 20 years. We employ experts in finishing, plating, machining, and casting. Our casting facility is a modern lost wax shell casting operation, which turns out essentially flawless product in yellow brass and red and white bronze. The castings are superb as a result of our casting technique, as well as our talented engineers who are responsible for the design of the product, the tooling, and the technique. Not all foundries are the same and this is one of the areas where Nanz is particularly outstanding. Hardware prior to our use of such casting methods had been a product, which was created via sand casting methods. The surface quality was far less desirable and the molds were highly dependent on the hand of the caster. Consequently, product varied greatly and quality levels were always in flux. Looking at the aerospace industry where quality was of the utmost importance, Nanz chose to incorporate lost wax shell casting to be the method of choice. It serves us well and is the reason why our product is preferred.

By employing traditional chasing techniques, textures resembling linen, burlap, sand, wood, grain or stone can be added to any product. Polished, burnished, satin, and patinated finishes can also be used to produce a nearly unlimited variety of custom finishes.

The Nanz Company

Only a handful of companies remain that can design and fabricate custom hardware. Full-size plastic prototypes are created in the Nanz studio in Soho, before being sent to the company's factory in Brooklyn to be fabricated and have custom finishes applied.
The Nanz Company

Our hand finishing techniques combined with our 3,000-square-foot (279-square-meter) electro plating line (another outstanding aspect of our operation) is also a matter that sets us apart. Early in our history, we were impressed with the time spent preparing our product for plating and we would outsource. Polishing, packaging, labeling, organizing, shipping, all these steps were time consuming and the results we got from our various platers were mixed, and lost or damaged product was a certainty. We decided to develop our own plating facility with a third-generation plater, who created and runs our current line. Continually updated with small improvements, our facility allows us the status of being the only competing manufacturer who does not source plating. It means Nanz maintains a level of finish quality that is really unmatchable.

The finest quality product is important to our success, but also essential are our adept project managers. It is these fellows who assure accurate specifications, bulletproof engineering, and trouble free installation.

More often than not these days, our project managers are invited to visit projects early in the process to work with the design team to help determine the best hardware solutions for a given project. It's a collaborative effort to ensure that the clients get the functional capabilities they desire in the most successful way possible.

Beautiful hardware manufactured to please. That's what we do and as a manufacturer with over a quarter of a century of experience, The Nanz Company has developed a broad range of great handles, locks and hinge designs for doors, cabinets, and windows. Combining the most modern casting and machining methods with traditional finishing techniques, we are making products indistinguishable from products fashioned in previous centuries—except that they work better, last longer, and each item is guaranteed for a lifetime. ❖

ABOVE:
This two knuckle lift-off butt hinge has a discreet bushing between each reeded knuckle, as well as acorn finials, all finished in antique bronze.
The Nanz Company

Architect Jeremy Dixon used this painting as a design tool to envision how his design for the Royal Opera House would fit into the busy fabric of Covent Garden, London.
Oil on Canvas by Carl Laubin

Collaborations with Dead Architects

Carl Laubin

My title derives from a comment made by the late great Modernist architectural perspectivist, Helmut Jacoby, when Derek Walker brought him to my studio a few years before he died. He looked around at the work on the walls, which was probably mainly of Palladian architecture, and said, "Very nice, but why do you only paint dead men's buildings?"

The temptation was to say, "Because they can't fight back," but I resisted and pointed out that I have had numerous enriching, productive, and enjoyable collaborations with living architects.

My relationship to collaborative work in an architectural team has been through many twists and turns over my career. Beginning as an architect who painted in my spare time, I was always part of an architectural team, which if I am honest, I was not particularly suited to, having a rather introverted character. So when Jeremy Dixon offered me the chance to apply my painting to projects in his office, it seemed an ideal situation to me. I would still be collaborating within an architectural team but also working on my own.

This slightly contradictory arrangement was reflected in the approach to the paintings for the Royal Opera House project. They were very much used as a design tool, highlighting areas that needed consideration and the paintings, in turn, changed continually as the design developed. This proved to be a definite advantage of oil painting over watercolor as repeated alteration was possible.

At the same time as the paintings were used to consider the design as part of a collaborative team effort, they also had a function as a detached observation. They were intended to look at how the buildings would age, weather and be used, even fail. They were not to be slick marketing images. Jeremy Dixon was exceptional in making use of the paintings as a design tool, feeling that the realism of the paintings showed up anything out of place in the architecture. As Jeremy later explained in an article in *Archives d'Architecture Moderne*, "The paintings were used to examine the effect on the appearance of various ideas. The paintings were so real that if anything looked wrong it had to be altered. One could not deceive oneself as so often happens. The paintings, therefore, became an integral part of the development of the project, a means of exploring the refinements of detail and style." (*Archives d'Architecture Moderne*, No. 40, 1990.) This in turn required an effort on my part to ensure the paintings did reflect as accurately as possible how the built work would appear. It was always important to Jeremy with Dudgeon's Wharf, for instance, that the project was seen "after a shower of rain," not pristinely with a brilliant blue sunny sky. To this end, I spent a long time studying the effects of rain on paving, trying to understand just how light penetrated down to the underlying surface in the shadows but reflected off the water in the sunlight. I remember thinking at the time, "I don't believe someone is actually paying me to study how to paint puddles!"

Similarly, I was struggling to understand how the openings in the colonnade vaulting of the Opera House would affect the light in the colonnades and took myself off to Florence to study the Uffizi colonnades on which the Opera House colonnades were modeled. On my return I scrapped my original version of the colonnade painting and began again with a better idea of the light reflected upwards onto the vaulting. This was one case where it was more beneficial to start again than to overpaint.

This use of the paintings to study the design was quite unique to Jeremy Dixon. Later collaborations with other architects could be equally intense but usually more in an attempt to get the painting to accurately reflect the intentions of the design than to affect it. In that sense, these collaborations were more related to later paintings of historical work, perhaps, where study of an architect's drawings led to a better understanding of, and ability to interpret, their work rather than to directly influence it. Working with John Outram, for instance, took quite a different direction. The paintings I did for him were not used to study the design and aid in its development, but rather to convey the allegorical nature of his buildings. This did require a very close collaboration for me to understand the complex symbolism incorporated in his architecture.

Another key aspect of the brief for the paintings developed with Jeremy, and one that I have always tried to adhere to when working for other architects, was that the paintings should depict a scene that an artist would have wanted to, or might have chosen to paint. That is, that architecture, particularly contemporary architecture when I was painting directly to commission for architects, was a fit subject for a work of art, that the painting should be worthy as a painting, not just a vehicle for promoting a design. And in that sense, it was a test for the building—would it stand up to that role and be as worthy a subject for a painting as an historic building would be. Often the building would not even be the subject of the painting, but part of the setting and this was in itself a test of whether or not the building fit into its environment. This was obviously a central consideration with a sensitive site like that of the Royal Opera House.

Having developed this approach with Jeremy Dixon, I went on to apply it to works by Léon Krier, John Outram, John Simpson, Quinlan Terry, Derek Walker, Benson and Forsyth, and Liam O'Connor among others.

The culmination of this work with contemporary architects must be my painting of the first decade of Driehaus Prize winners, *A Classical Perspective*, which combined the work of 10 contemporary architects in one imaginary landscape. There was little actual collaboration with the architects on this painting but a great deal of time spent familiarizing myself with the various architects' work, much of it new to me, choosing the projects to be represented and trying to skip convincingly between the differing architectural styles represented.

Viewing architecture as a suitable subject for a work of art (no doubt coinciding with the rise in computer-generated images) led to doing less work directly for architects, a wider interest in architectural subject matter, and fascination with the architectural *capriccio*.

I do not think working less with contemporary architects necessarily involved ceasing architectural collaboration. In creating a *capriccio* of the work of an architect no longer living, one is denied direct instruction on how to proceed, but that perhaps means one must work even harder to find a collaboration, an understanding of their motives and intentions. This is particularly true when trying to create an image of a work that was never built or has been destroyed, and one is forced to work just from the drawings as if working for an architect intending to build a new work. This has happened with paintings of the architecture of Wren, Hawksmoor, Vanbrugh, Cockerell, Palladio, and especially Ledoux. In each case it has been necessary to become immersed in their drawings to understand how to reconstruct their works. But there is also a collaboration involved in painting an existing building; in trying to be receptive to the architect's intentions when walking around it and allowing oneself to be guided by the architecture and to become lost in someone else's "built idea".

I am especially aware of this having just completed a *capriccio* of the work of Sir Edwin Lutyens, *Metiendo Vivendum*. This includes a number of buildings that were not built, the demolished Papillon Hall and Cheyne Walk, and several buildings to which I was unable to gain access, so that I was forced to rely solely on drawings in many cases to construct an image. There were also many existing buildings I could visit, some with very specific connections to their sites that needed to be understood and reflected in the painting. So there was a wide range of building designs that had to be related to in very different ways but hopefully ending up with a consistent degree of presence in the painting.

The major challenge in *Metiendo Vivendum* was to depict Lutyens's unbuilt Liverpool Cathedral. There is a model that was built to be shown at the Royal Academy in 1933. There are numerous exhibition drawings done at the same time as the model, and later drawings produced for the Lutyens Memorial Volumes, documenting his work and produced after his death. All of these contain contradictory information; but most importantly there is Thiepval, the Memorial to the Missing of the Somme, which embodies many of the design issues pertinent to the cathedral. It is a key to understanding Lutyens's thinking in relation to the cathedral and I could not have constructed a believable image of the cathedral without seeing Thiepval. Both derive their form from sequences of arches descending in size in alternating directions and in detail both have surfaces that react minutely to accommodate the very minimal applied detail such as the band thickness of the arches. It is in the various setbacks in the façades of Thiepval that Lutyens shows us how the surfaces of the cathedral would have been manipulated.

As to the contradictions between the various drawings and the model, I think the realization that Lutyens hardly ever built anything completely

according to the drawings, without altering it on site, adds authority to the model. I believe he would have taken an interest in the model's construction and in seeing its realization of the drawings—in much the same way as he would have taken inspiration from the emergence of form witnessed on a building site—and altered the drawn design accordingly. There are areas of brickwork shown at the main parapet/aedicule level on the model, which are indicated as stone in both the drawings done for the Royal Academy and the later Memorial Volumes drawings. There are also additional window openings at the level below this on the model that do not appear in the drawings. I do not imagine the model maker put these in on his own initiative.

I was reinforced in this opinion on the precedence the model should probably take by Gavin Stamp. This brings me to another aspect of collaboration that was important to *Metiendo Vivendum*, with individuals who have studied his work, written about him or lived in or worked on his buildings. Reading Gavin Stamp, John Summerson, Pevsner, Lawrence Weaver, Christopher Hussey, A. S. G. Butler, Roderick Gradidge and others about Lutyens's architecture, and Mary Lutyens, Jane Ridley, and Jane Brown about the man, was part of a year and a half of total immersion in Lutyens. Further insights and clues were provided by Michael Edwards who has done restoration and extension work on numerous Lutyens houses and by many owners, gardeners, and managers of properties I visited, all helping to piece together an idea of the man and his buildings.

I believe it was a genuine collaboration, gathering information from as many diverse sources as possible, all interested in giving as complete a picture as possible of an aspect of the man's architecture. The variety of sources was crucial in the case of Lutyens where there are so many and diverse veins to his work. Many individuals know him for a particular area of his work, few for the totality of it. The aim of the painting was to give an impression of this totality. In my opinion, Lutyens was the J. S. Bach of architecture. A workaholic, prolific with creative invention pouring out of him; an obsession with proportion and order; a master of the mathematical and the technical but also of humanizing his art, giving it emotional impact. Only collaboration with the widest variety of sources could give a complete understanding of his work. It is an example of collaboration building a much richer picture than would be possible without utilizing the enormous knowledge and expertise of others. ❦

PAGES 98 - 99:
Metiendo Vivendum (By Measure We live) depicts the work of Sir Edwin Lutyens in the form of a capriccio. The composition is dominated by Lutyens unrealized design for Liverpool Cathedral. Rather than create a scene in perspective to minimize its impact, Carl Laubin instead choice to place the Cathedral in the center of the canvas and paint each and every building at 1:200 scale – highlighting the sheer volume, scale, and variety of Lutyens work.
Oil on Canvas by Carl Laubin

OPPOSITE:
Dudgeon's Wharf: Depicting a new waterfront housing development in London's docklands, architect Jeremy Dixon insisted that the scene be captured after a rain shower.
Oil on Canvas by Carl Laubin

Inside the London showroom of Pentreath & Hall is an eclectic mix of antique and modern furniture, pictures, books, and living accessories – highlighting the owners own preferences, and only selling things that they would buy themselves.
Ben Pentreath Ltd.

Building Today

Ben Pentreath

In her brilliant novel *The Fountainhead*, Ayn Rand brought to life the tortured, powerful, ego-driven architect-manqué Howard Roarke. Ever since, the popular perception of architecture has been shaped by the idea of the individual genius, the angry romantic artist, struggling to make forms of great importance and unique appearance in a world that does not understand them. Architecture is seen as the practice of the lonely artist. Roarke knew the power of unadorned structure, collaborated with his builder and foreman, but made few other friends along the way.

The architect Francis Terry (who also writes in this book) has been known to quote an altogether softer line, and it is one that I love. "Fortune favors the friendly," he says, turning on its head that old adage, "Fortune favors the bold." I've never been convinced entirely of the sense of that line; it seems to me that the bold are very often first over the line, and subsequently the first to get shot. And increasingly, I realize, the creation of beautiful architecture is a matter of making friends. It's a giant collaboration. This is in the *Zeitgeist*. Valentina Rice, the New York-based founder of *Many Kitchens*, a successful collaborative of small-batch artisan food producers, gave a recent *TED Talk* entitled 'Why competition is so last century: building a non-competitive community of artisans in an Amazon world.'

A lot has been written about the role of patronage in architecture, and I'm sure that it goes without saying that the greatest collaborations are ones where the patron-architect relationship pushes each to greater results. Sandy Stoddard, the esteemed neo-Classical sculptor, once said to me, "Clients merely get the building they want. Patrons get the work of art they deserve." This is true. The patron is someone with enough money to do the job well— but not too much. And someone who—like your best friends—has respect for others, a sense of their own humility, a belief in the dignity of others... and, above all, a brilliant sense of humor. Because what is life if we can't have a good laugh at it, and what is architecture if it's not a reflection of life? I'm very scared of architects or, for that matter, clients who take themselves too seriously. As I'm heard to mutter from time to time, when things go wrong and the world appears to be collapsing, "No one died." Sometimes you wonder if the late arrival of a robe hook on a bathroom door is an equivalent event to the declaration of World War III, but that is perhaps a story for another day.

For me, positive collaborations extend in so many more directions. They start in my office. I run a small office based in Bloomsbury, in the heart of 18th-century London. We've grown slowly over the last decade, and with me have grown people who have a specific and tremendous aptitude for the various tasks at hand. Rob Illingworth is "Master-Planning Man." Rupert Cunningham is the "Country House" department. A remarkable team assists them and we work with friends as well.

In one of our urban design projects, Poundbury, the Prince of Wales's extension of Dorchester, I work alongside a superb and dedicated group of individuals at the Duchy of Cornwall; and specifically very closely alongside the architect George Saumarez Smith (whose work is also featured in this book), whom I have known for years. When we are asked to work on projects that are more contemporary in character, I often collaborate with another colleague, William Smalley. He's modernist, I'm traditional. We both meet in the middle and the results can be inspiring for both of us. Across the street, meanwhile, in our decoration department, Luke Edward Hall and Lucy Wilks run the softest, most comfortable (but most tightly operated) interior design firm that you can imagine. Or in our shop, based around the corner, we collaborate with artists and makers on a weekly basis. Last year, I sold half of the shop to my collaborator and partner Bridie Hall, and it grows from strength to strength as a result. Really, this entire essay should be dedicated to Zoe Wightman, who runs the whole studio, and makes sure it operates as smoothly as you could imagine.

Over the years I've built up incredible relationships with many people who I have come to depend on. We have a shared language and common understanding that makes the process of design both nimble and enjoyable. Somehow, I'm able still to feel that I design every building or interior that leaves the office. But in a great part this is because I surround myself with people who are talented, happy, and reliable. I used to think that if I wanted something really well done, I had better do it myself. I am now sensible enough to realize that if I want something really well done, I had better do it with others. There is a power in numbers—not too many, not too few.

The role of collaboration in architecture extends across disciplines. Tried and trusted mechanical or structural engineers are the difference between the mechanics of a house being a trial or a pleasure to design and conceive. The fragmentation of the discipline of architecture into a million different elements responds to the increasing complexity of houses—literally, they have become machines to live in, in the early 21st century. Pulling the strands together again requires effort or, in a different way; the building needs a considered and beautifully designed setting. We work with brilliant landscape architects and designers with whom I love working—in particular, Kim Wilkie and Pip Morrison. On many projects I ask clients for their involvement on day one, where we begin to place buildings and forms within the landscape together.

At the moment, some of the greatest collaborations I enjoy are with makers and builders. As I write, we are half way through the construction of a great new country house in a quiet village in Oxfordshire, not far from Henley. Here, we are reconstructing and rebuilding a small, early Georgian house (c1715) and creating something altogether new from its bones. The house is being built by a local firm of builders, Symm, founded just 100 years after Fawley House

A computer rendering of a new house in the south of England.
The design is based upon Cronkhill, a famous Picturesque
Italianate villa designed by Regency architect Sir John Nash.
Ben Pentreath Ltd.

The sitting room of Ben Pentreath's own house, located in an
early nineteenth-century parsonage in rural Dorset.
Ben Pentreath Ltd.

Founded in 2008 by architect Ben Pentreath, Pentreath & Hall is a small shop in the heart of Bloomsbury that has become one of the most influential stores in the London decoration world.

was first built. Symm brings together an extraordinary number of craftsmen and women. Bricklayers, masons, leadworkers, and roofers pay the same attention to their disciplines as do stone carvers, joiners, woodcarvers, metalworkers, cabinetmakers, and painters. Each in their own way brings their craft and skill to bear on each element of our building. Together, their skills conjoin into a building where the whole is growing into something far greater than the sum of their parts. The sense of shared effort extends from the client to the groundworker digging trenches, and all the way to the real conductor of the piece—the site foreman Bob Scrivens. He is the person who brings together the various strands of the great orchestra

involved in the construction, over years, of a building like this. He makes sure that the woodwind, violins, and drums play at precisely the right moment, neither too hard, nor too soft.

I guess in this analogy, I'm the composer, but the point of everything I've just written is that the composition is itself a form of collaboration between people, as much as it is between our own moment in time, and the past, and the future. This process is very special. I think it is unique in the world of the creative arts, stepping as it does, and always has, between the triumvirate of "firmness, commodity, and delight." And it is why I love architecture. ⚜

This historic 1724 brick house in the Brandywine River Valley
was carefully restored and expanded. The addition, clad in dark
brown clapboard siding, includes a new kitchen on the first floor
and a master bedroom suite above.
John Milner Architects

Design and Preservation

John Milner

When my wife Wynne and I were planning to restore and expand our brick house, dating back to 1724 in Pennsylvania's Brandywine River Valley, we engaged a team of archeologists to investigate the area to be impacted by new construction. We discovered the foundations of two earlier buildings and a scattering of artifacts relating to the site's historic and prehistoric occupation. Wynne was teaching gifted children in a local middle school and invited one of her students with an interest in archeology to assist with the excavations. His mother dropped him off on a warm summer morning and he was immediately put to work carrying buckets of dirt to the sifting screen. After about an hour of soiled jeans and moderate perspiration, the young man announced that he had decided to teach archeology. An interesting concept, as I have always favored practice over theory.

My background in both design and historic preservation has given me a profound appreciation for the importance of collaboration with one's peers in the pursuit of a successful and rewarding venture. Very early on, I teamed with archeologists and historians to expand the base of knowledge about historic sites. Understanding when, how and why buildings and their environs evolved over time is critical to their responsible stewardship. The excavations at our house revealed fragments of lead strips and very old window glass which, when matched with the physical evidence in the masonry wall openings, confirmed the existence of original leaded glass windows as referenced in historical accounts. A significant aspect of our restoration project was replacement of the modern windows with exact reproductions of the original units.

My interest in architecture flowed from my fascination with the craftsmanship employed in making buildings. An internship with the Historic American Buildings Survey was invaluable in understanding the many parts of a building and how they were fabricated and assembled. For me, one of the important parts of the design and construction process is establishing and maintaining a dialog with the craftsmen engaged in a project. Putting myself in the mind of the craftsman allows me to make a direct connection between concept and execution. That exercise is constantly applied with the restoration of historic buildings, because it is so important to follow the logic of the craftsman as he resolved complex details in executing the overall design intent. This information becomes a part of our firm's archive of precedents that serves us well, not only for other restoration projects, but also for the design of new buildings.

When contemplating a design in stone, we visit the quarry with our clients to review the range of options for available materials, understand their geological characteristics, and select the most appropriate approach to achieving the aesthetic objective. The stone that we commonly use in new construction is referred to by quarrymen as "free stone" because it exists in the subsoil, above the deeper bedrock as separate pieces, and is extracted by surface excavation. This material gains color and character through various degrees of interaction with the soil and the air. Free stone can also be called "field stone," because it was turned up and set aside in rows by farmers as they plowed their fields. It can be shaped to fit specific applications by hand or by cutting machines called guillotines. The relatively small sizes facilitate installation in a wall. For larger buildings and for more specialized applications, the solid bedrock can be extracted in large sections and cut into prescribed sizes. The handling of this material is more challenging than with the "free stone."

Whenever possible, it is prudent to include the contractor and mason in the selection process, since they can provide valuable guidance and will be responsible for dressing and installing the material. Once the selection is made, we then work with the contractor and mason to construct a temporary section of wall that incorporates typical conditions such as stone pattern, mortar configuration and color, outside corners, window openings, eaves, and decorative features. This also provides a convenient opportunity to select colors and textures for adjacent features like woodwork and roofing. Occasionally, our designs incorporate antique features which are carefully integrated with the walls built of local stone.

When designing a building in brick, there are abundant options for size, texture, color, pattern, and mortar configuration. The physical characteristics and appearance of brick is influenced by the clay deposits from which it is made, admixtures that are specified, and the process by which the units are shaped, cured and fired. All of these variables make brick a fascinating material, which affords both beauty and permanence to works of architecture. Brick samples are easily transported to a project location to be reviewed in the context of a particular setting and assembled in a temporary panel for experimentation and approval. Collaboration with the brick mason is essential in realizing the full potential of the material and its installation. The mason's experience with, and knowledge of, the intricacies of fine brickwork can make a significant contribution to the final composition. A great deal of pre-planning and "lay-out" is required to insure that the desired bonding pattern of the wall surface can be achieved and is coordinated with building corners, window and door placement and integral decorative features.

Whenever possible, we encourage collaboration with Landscape Architects who share our vision for settling our buildings into the site. Making the architecture at one with its environment creates so many opportunities for interaction, enhancing the enjoyment of both.

A common thread in the design of interior spaces in historic houses is the hierarchy of detail, which defined function and relative importance of the spaces. In a simple or grand house of the 18th, 19th, and early 20th century, primary emphasis in terms of architectural embellishment was placed on the spaces where visitors would be received and entertained. For instance, the entrance hall with a stairway, living

ON POINT FARM (see page 185): The interior of this new home is organized by a central linear axis that joins all of the formal rooms, and incorporates antiques acquired by the architect for their clients.
John Milner Architects

For the past forty years John Milner architects has worked with The Chadds Ford Historical Society to ensure the long-term preservation and conservation of this 1714 English-built tavern.

room and dining room would have the highest level of detail in woodwork and other finishes. The details would be simplified in rooms of lesser importance, and become quite plain in the service areas. In our design of new houses we endeavor to carry on the hierarchical tradition, often with subtle distinctions in the treatment of individual rooms.

I have been intrigued with architectural woodwork ever since I was doing research in the 1960s at the Library Company of Philadelphia for a restoration project with which I was involved, and discovered *The Rules for Drawing the Several Parts of Architecture* (James Gibbs, 1732). This is one of a number of architectural pattern books published in England during the 18th century and used by designers and builders in the colonies for inspiration and guidance. Using a series of illustrative plates with written instructions, Gibbs set forth a methodology for drawing the classical orders, establishing ideal proportional relationships between the parts, and creating profiles for individual moldings.

I was also captivated by the exuberant woodwork found in vernacular 18th-century houses in southeastern Pennsylvania. Carefully examining the details of design and assembly of these compositions connected me with the craftsmen, and compelled me to follow their lead by collaborating with skilled woodworkers to produce new compositions soundly influenced by historical precedent.

The most rewarding projects with the best results are those that have had the benefit of collegial and collaborative relationships among clients, designers, builders, and craftsmen. Design is the first step, but the craftsmen's contributions are fundamental to realizing, enriching and giving personality to a final creation. ❧

ABOVE:
ON POINT FARM (see page 185): The mudroom in this new house, evokes old-world charm with a fireplace effortlessly integrated into the painted wood paneling.
John Milner Architects

Antique mirrored glass lines the chimney breast and slips of the fireplace, giving the otherwise traditional architecture a modern playful twist, and uniting it with the eclectic mix of furnishings.

Lynne Scalo Design

Creation and Connection

Lynne Scalo

Collaboration, very simply, is in our DNA. The first prehistoric cave paintings, dating to the Paleolithic Era/Old Stone Age were discovered in Altamira, Spain in the late 1800s. These 18,000-year-old drawings tell the story of that time and are of supreme artistic quality. As an interior designer, I am in the position to tell a story through art and interiors. My desire to always be in contact with art and then bring it to the environment that surrounds us is what makes my profession such an integral part of modern times. Instead of caves, I use interiors of homes to tell the story of the individuals living within them, through a collaboration vision – both my client's and my own.

One of my earliest childhood memories involves my mother – herself a gifted artist – reading me a bedtime story, or rather showing me photos, and telling me the basic principles of design. Mom showed me photos of Frank Lloyd Wright's Fallingwater house in Pennsylvania. "Form follows function" was one of the earliest imprints in my life.

For me, creating an environment is an artistic process. Being surrounded by art itself is, I believe, the culmination of a project. With this, not only do I mean great paintings but unique architecture, furniture, and textile designs that can talk amongst themselves is what a designer-created environment provides to a space. Architectural design goes hand in hand with an aesthetic collaboration of the interiors. Architecture and interior design are a combination making the design whole. Without one the other could not exist.

I believe that there is no expiration date in great design – each epoch has its elements that can be carried forward until the end of time. Fully understanding the history of architecture, art, furniture, and its impact on culture is critical to my craft of interior design. I often explain this to my clients. For example, the klismos chair, created by the ancient Greeks and perfected in the 5th century BC, is still visible in our designs, only reimagined in brass and woven earth-tone leather making it shockingly modern. It would be perfectly at home displayed in the MOMA (Museum of Modern Art). Beauty transcends time and designing a home requires integrating each period to modern life. I create homes within which people can love their lives.

I have had the privilege of working with quite a few well-versed masters who are each proficient in their field. These architects, artisans, artists, and landscape designers are my partners in design and each brings a unique school of thought to the design process.

The art of interior design is innately a collaborative effort. It is foremost informed by the client creating a background in which they live their lives.

Empowerment is a by-product of self-expression. Therefore, the experience of collaborating with my clients ends up being an experience that empowers each client with the knowledge they have helped make their space just that – "their space." I have found that I have grown my own very distinct and well-informed point of view, which I credit to leading to my recognition and accolades in my own field of interior design.

In my initial meetings with clients I find that as long as I come with an open mind I can often glean inspiration that will set me off on the best path to exceed their expectations. Whether my client is new to the process of working with an interior designer or a seasoned expert on interior design also plays a part in how the process will play itself out. I love when a client can give me a few hints as to their aesthetic but they are also looking to me and my artistic ability to create their dream home.

My design process evolves with each client relationship. The depth and breadth of each project determines how the collaborative nature will enhance the goals of each home being created. There are times that a project comes to me with nothing more than a set of blueprints. This gets me so excited because I know I can literally be in on the ground floor and work with my client, their architect, their builders, craftsmen, and landscape designers to bring my client's dream home to fruition. The collaborative nature of such a project gives me the opportunity to glean inspiration from each artist involved. Yes I consider the creation of a home to be the ultimate art. We are fortunate enough to live in a time and place where the home can be a place not just providing shelter and the basics but serves as a retreat from the daily business of life.

Architecture plays a huge role in my design process. Once the architecture has been identified I work with my clients to help them visualize themselves within their new home to be. It helps when they have an idea of their personal style but quite often I have families moving from an urban environment to the suburbs for the first time. This can be overwhelming, especially when coming from a small space to a large home with a vast outdoor space. My first goal is to reassure and encourage all involved – meeting the entire family actually is very important to me – even the pets! I want to know who will be in the space and how it will be used. Family life is a constant collaboration and the space within the home needs to be one that fosters time together, as well as providing retreats for each family member.

My style is also a collaboration in another sense – not just among individuals but among historical periods. I love, love, love, to blend the new with the classical. Did I say love? There are reasons that certain looks and pieces stand the test of time – because they are perfect. One of my secrets is to design and create a desk and instead of using leather as an inlay (which would be expected) I will use mirrors. This sort of combination adds just the right amount of glamour to make a classic shape just modern enough to also stand the test of time.

The most exciting part of every project for me is the installation phase. The excitement and energy is palpable and serves as the culmination of months

A Chandelier of striped glass spheres hangs at various heights, providing a changing focal point as one ascends and descends the staircase.
Lynne Scalo Design

This living room is the epitome of successfully mixing old and new. Here a Chippendale mirror, Klismos chair, a custom designed sofa all fit together in a classically detailed room.
Lynne Scalo Design

Reminiscent of a classic English design, yet with a modern twist that has become Lynne Scalo's forte, the custom sofa in this living room is tufted inside and out and bowed to envelope its sitter.

of work – and waiting – between myself, my clients, the architects, and other craftsman. It's a process of layering, beginning with the walls and floors, then furnishings, and last but not least what is commonly referred to as the final *zhush*. This word dates back as far as 1968 in Britain. It was the American Dialect Society 2003 "Word of the Year" and is defined as a verb meaning to "primp or fluff up." This stage is somewhat undervalued in many clients' minds until they see it happening before their eyes. The movement of an object by as little as 2 inches can change the feeling in a space and combining my artistic eye with the need for the functionality of the room make for a really fun process of "zhushing."

When I first opened my firm almost 15 years ago I knew I had a lot to learn. I also knew I had the heart and soul to put myself into growing my passion beyond my wildest dreams. These past years have instilled in me the knowledge that I have so many resources to call upon that no project is off limits to me. As I open the doors to my new atelier in Greenwich, Connecticut, this year, I welcome the opportunity to expand my reach and continue to build upon existing relationships and grow new ones. Greenwich is home to many artisanal masters in the home-design field – including the author of this book – and I am so enjoying this next phase of creating a collaborative symphony of professional artists. ❦

Henry fittings and Grove Brickworks transition between modern
and traditional, straightforward but not over-simplified.
Waterworks

Vision, Voice and Viability

Barbara Sallick

Thirty-six years and counting—that is the length of time I have collaborated with my family. First with my husband and then my son—and colleagues to shape an industry, create a sustainable and respected business, forge lasting relationships with staff, clients and factories, and design memorable objects. Through the years, I have learned that a successful collaboration is truly an art form. It requires that multiple parties and personalities bring their unique perspectives to the table and work together to solve a problem. They must become aligned in their vision, develop a common language to direct the creative process and have procedures in place for working through many steps and challenges until goals are achieved.

Obviously, this can be tricky business. I have found that the best way to bring all the collaborators and all the pieces together is to have a clear, in-depth and honest story of inspiration and purpose. That is how you get everyone on the same page from the start. Then, it is essential that each participant have an investment in the outcome of the venture. For a collaboration is also the balance of artistic endeavors and fiscal responsibility. There needs to be a willingness to set realistic expectations and refer to them as the guiding principles for the desired outcome, otherwise it is easy to get derailed.

The very first step is to bring an idea (or several) to the table. I am often asked where the spark for a particular design came from. It varies: sometimes it comes from a photo, an experience, a conversation; and other times it may be inspired by fashion, travel or an object sitting on a desk. One example of a random inspiration is the story behind the design of the Roadster fitting from Waterworks Studio. One day at our offices in Connecticut, my design collaborator and I were discussing the charms of Benton Egee, a local country doctor. We both admired his good taste, fabulous bowties and all of his vintage cars, particularly his 1950s MG. The creation of Roadster was underway. As always, one thing leads to another and our process prompted us to change our original direction, get online to research details and imagine what that car's designer might have created if he designed a fitting. The end result wasn't exactly what we first imagined (it rarely is), but when you look carefully at the Roadster escutcheon and the scale of the handle, you will easily recognize the dashboard and steering wheel of that classic car.

A credible story or inspiration is the start of a great collaboration. It defines the right problem to solve and its clarity is a way to include and inform everyone—from designers and engineers to manufacturers and sales consultants—involved with the project. Telling a compelling story allows for honest conversations about style and context, it provides vocabulary for discussing design and creates opportunity to establish reference points for inspiration. Ultimately, it is the navigational tool that efficiently directs clients to the most appropriate product.

When Waterworks looks for the influence of an outside designer to bring fresh thinking and expertise to the creation of a new fittings family or collection, it is imperative that the collaborator embraces the responsibility, respect and reputation of the brand. We look for smart, dedicated designers who are willing to learn a new language and worry about how things work as well as how they look. Sometimes the person is well known, other times we choose someone on the cusp of a breakthrough. But always, the collaboration needs to yield results where the outcomes are unfaltering in all of the benchmarks for successful design thinking. Together, we need to deliver a product that is viable and consistent with our well-established brand message.

The process of creating a bath fitting is a unique experience for most designers. It is a functional, mechanical and permanent piece of equipment that must deliver water in a reliable, pleasing and humanistic way. It is also expensive. We don't have the luxury of making a mistake; unlike a chair or window treatment, fittings cannot be easily banished to the next yard sale. Financial and practical considerations—from the cost of making the tools, to the ease of plating, assembling and polishing— factor into the final design decisions. Our design collaborators learn quickly about the constraints and

costs of creating complex molds and tools that result in a lifetime investment. Often compromise is part of the process in order to deliver a product that is a viable, commercial entity.

In addition to working with outside design collaborators, there are a number of others whose expertise is necessary to complete a design-driven project. We have our in-house engineering team that takes the wire frame drawings and turns them into 3-D models. The cross-functional product development and inventory management teams select the appropriate factories, create line lists, cost spreadsheets, projections and place orders. And the sales and marketing teams help present the finished product to the world. We all work in tandem through a discovery process to establish a working protocol for identifying the right tactics, attributes, timelines, and strategies to create a product whose quality, value and relevance will be consistent over decades.

The design and manufacturing collaboration can be years long with countless touch points over time. One of our newest collections took more than three years to develop. Along the way, we had to let go of some ideas, rework others and compromise on even more. That is one reason why we have to fall madly in love with a concept in the design stage, otherwise we may not be able to push through the engineering, manufacturing and production challenges to make it happen. Our mission is to create an aesthetic that is desirable to a lot of people. But, making pretty, beautiful, timeless, and sophisticated objects is meaningless if we cannot make the fitting work!

This computer design rendering shows the assemble of parts for the Henry three hole faucet set with metal cross handles.
Waterworks

The ultimate goal of a Waterworks collaboration is to deliver a powerful client experience. This is achieved by understanding how to make the right choices, create possibilities, choose direction, and execute within the constraints of time and resources. We think about design as a tool for solving problems and discovering new opportunities; this is the foundation for driving our brand and consistently meeting our clients' needs. Through our 36-plus years of collaborating within and outside of the company, we have realized success by keeping an open mind, taking risks, sweating the details, and not being afraid to recalibrate until we get it absolutely right.

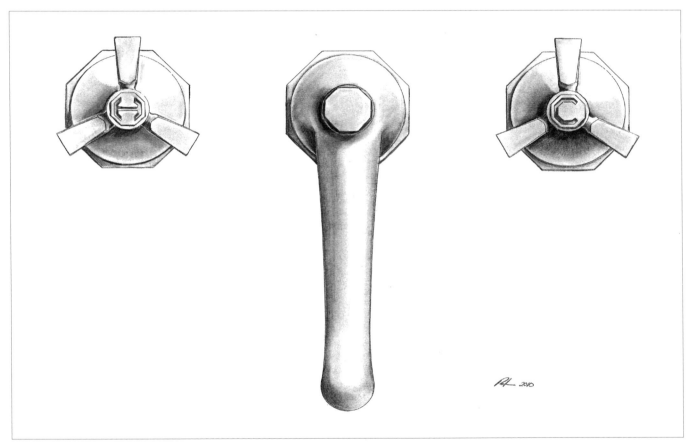

OPPOSITE:
The inspiration board for Waterworks "Henry Collection" shows how innovation begins with the translation and evolution of ideas. Influenced by modernist and industrial age thinking, Waterworks created geometric angles with deep curves and sleek marble and teak gland cover options to create a fitting with deep modernist origins and character, yet inherently and timelessly fluid.

ABOVE:
The design sketch for Waterworks "Roadster Collection" is reminiscent of the dashboard of a streamlined vintage sports car, with octagonal indices and geometric shapes.

Students of The American College of the Building Arts in Charleston, South Carolina, learn the traditional time-tested skills of applying plaster and stucco.

The Academic Experiment

William Bates III

After World War II, programs like the G.I. Bill afforded college education to a huge number of formerly unknown, and apprenticeships and enrollment in traditional trade schools began a steady decline. More and more people flooded to a perceived ideal education – the white-collar job – and in so doing advanced a negative stigma on the subject of craft.

Postwar modernists promoting all things traditional as obsolete, if not heretical, seized on the decline of craft to support their grip on the architecture of America. Modernists promoted that people no longer needed traditional ways of construction, no longer needed soul-feeding ornament. 'Less is more." Those that could perform in the traditional ways were slowly pushed out of the marketplace and into professional career paths. With fewer and fewer craftsmen to understand and build the obsolete methods, a self-fulfilling deterioration ensued.

I suggest that the lack of need has more to do with the lack of understanding. It is very easy to dismiss something as unnecessary if you do not understand it. No one promotes a skill they do not possess.

As fewer and fewer people understood the reasons for these traditional methods it furthered the case of the modernists. Struggling through the Dark Ages of the 1950s and 1960s, my then future friend Henry Hope

Reed and his band of classicists held the banner off the ground while it took the rest of America over 30 years for the problems with the modernist agenda to crystallize. Slowly, beginning in the 1970s, more and more people began to recognize the issue with the wholesale dismissal of a craft-based education. I first noticed some hope with the publications of the *Foxfire Book* series, a subtle mixture of oral history, folklore and how-to. People were recognizing that if old methods were not preserved they would drop out of our cultural memory, lost to time. Through the 1980s and 1990s, other groups like the Institute of Classical Architecture and Art, determined to provide a safe haven for these fuddy-duddies, stayed, expanded and advanced the course of traditional methods with their teachings.

I first became acquainted with our predecessor organization, founded in the late 90s, the School of the Building Arts, through its founder. Intrigued with his ideas I questioned why a trade school would only offer trade classes. My conception early on was to offer parallel coursework in proportion, ratio, geometric construction, sketching, design, and drawing. These concepts were not so different from what any tradesmen of a prior, but not too distant age, would have known. If classicism plays a fundamental role in every age of the built environment then so too must the craftspeople who build it. Their education in these time-honored methods is as critical to the survival of classicism as academic and philosophical pursuits. After a few years of pressing the point, the idea of transforming the school into a four-year liberal arts college gained speed through their board. There appeared to be room for my ideas, alongside many others, in this "liberal arts meets trade school" incubator. An academic experiment began to take shape.

We all came together with the intent of creating the first licensed four-year liberal arts college of the building arts in America, and so we did. We began with some concerns and questions.

If the accepted method of apprenticeship could leave the student knowing a lot about one subject their master artisan was really good at, say stone carving, but lacking in another, say business skills, the student was at the mercy of any master artisan's biggest weakness. Could we remove that risk from the apprenticeship model by assembling a group of well-versed professors in a whole range of trade skills and liberal arts? If by following the collegiate model of the liberal arts, grammar, rhetoric, logic, arithmetic, could we collaborate with enough masters in one place to minimize the gaps?

Could we produce well-rounded artisans that could not only create hand-crafted objects sensitive to their surroundings but also be prepared with a business plan, foreign language skills and a keen sense of the differences and similarities of Pythagoras and Palladio? Could the continuation of time-honored and historically vetted instruction like architectural history and hand drafting – now rarely taught at the college level – be combined with historic preservation, architectural design and computer aided drafting?

Could this create a program so unique in America that it would change the course of how trades are perceived and perpetuated into the next century? How would this collaboration change the way buildings are built?

For about 18 months, the esteemed board, founding professors and administrators toiled over the best methods of answering those questions. First, to create an environment in which to teach students the fundamentals of being a well-rounded artisan – English taught with a bent toward the built, mathematics with application in the everyday world of the job site, foreign language in a builder's voice. Business classes creating graduates that can write a business plan, create an invoice, and balance a checkbook. When we sorted through the ideas, a plan was in place for our first incoming class in the Fall of 2005.

So that was the beginning of the American College of the Building Arts, now a decade along. The trials of creating a college none of us knew, and thankfully so, as we may not have attacked the idea with quite the vigor and zeal required for such an amazing endeavor. Since then I have promoted the idea that beauty is in fact not in the eye of the beholder, which we may debate on a different page, but the differences between a well-crafted object and a poorly crafted one are lost on no one who can interact both. Those differences are fundamental. Building a support group of people who understand the difference has debunked some of the stigmatic myths of modernism. Development of the college has – I suppose like any – never ceased to evolve, but the fundamentals of those first ideas have stayed strong.

In reflection, this past decade educating the students – eager to learn something that has not been taught in American schools in decades and never taught at the four-year college level – actually proved easy. Eagerness parallels absorption rate. Educating everyone else, however, proved to be a large but essential part in the ever-present need for funding a private not-for-profit college. When approaching someone for financial support often the question was, "Why is this important?" In an age where few people grew up with plaster walls I was always surprised to hear people who thought they had plaster walls when in fact they had sheetrock. "What's the difference?" they would ask and I would extol the insulative, fire and mold-resistant properties of hand plaster as well as the tactile qualities and the soft visual subtleties of a hand-plastered wall. In an age where few people grew up with wrought iron I was always surprised to hear people who thought they had wrought iron when in fact they had extruded aluminum, albeit black. "What's the difference?" they would ask. I would extol the structural and physical beauties of hand-wrought iron over that of extruded aluminum with its dull details all mechanically coerced, and high-embodied energy, which is so bad for our environment. Even the nuance of hand-carved stone ornament over that of cast stone was lost on most of the people I have encountered throughout the development of the college. However, once one sees the enthusiastic results of the students work, they not only never ask about the difference again but also seem to revel in explaining the difference to anyone else who will stop to listen.

One of the goals of the college was to educate on the subject of the restoration and preservation of ancient dwellings. Charleston, South Carolina, is a living laboratory where one can see the built environment under constant siege, and she is the perfect place to learn and apply these time-honored methods to keep her and other historic cities vital. New construction, however, has proved a great ally of the college with the world's growing concern for our environment. Not only does traditional construction assure the growth of these crafts, as they are perhaps the greenest sort of green, but they provide our graduates with an even broader landscape for their skillset. As residential patrons are the lion's share of those interested in ancient crafts and craftspeople, building relationships between the educated client, the educated designer and the educated craftsperson will do more to ensure the perpetuation of these methods than anything else we can do.

The college was founded on the principal of collaboration between theory and practice, on craft and the liberal arts. This is not an insular gathering of skills. We teach the importance of collaboration across trades, with clients and with a design team. In this way, we can promote the classical by building in that tradition, where the method is integral to the final result. No one promotes a skill they do not possess. As such, the preceding essays in this book will prove to be a valuable resource not only for our students, but also for all of those who appreciate the artistry of the building arts. ❧

PART II

THE PROJECTS

A SEASIDE RESIDENCE
HAMPSHIRE, ENGLAND

Nigel Anderson, ADAM Architecture

This house is on the Hampshire shoreline near Beaulieu, in the south of England, and is located beside its own private beach with panoramic views across the Solent to the Isle of Wight. It is the third house to have been built on the site in less than 30 years and replaces a nondescript building that did little justice to the dramatic setting.

The owners wanted a comfortable and informal home that took full advantage of the views and the ever-changing weather conditions. The inspiration for the design was a fusion of the campagna villas designed by John Nash and the later "butterfly" plans of the Arts and Crafts movement. The former gives an air of informality and acknowledges the Regency seaside architecture found elsewhere along the south coast. The latter allows most of the main rooms to have a triple aspect. A series of intimate courtyard garden areas are on all sides of the house, which can be used at various times of the day and also provide shelter from the strong winds when the weather is less than clement.

The ground floor interior has a free-flowing series of interconnected living spaces with few separating doors. The principal rooms face onto the beach and the Solent. Large areas of glazing bring together the interior and exterior spaces, as well as the wider views beyond. The double-height dining hall acts as a circulation hub at both floor levels. The circular stair hall has a cantilevered stone staircase and a domed ceiling. Further stairs lead to the rooftop and a comfortable seated viewing platform.

The owner of the house, Chief Executive of one of the UK's largest construction companies, and his wife, had previously built homes in the Caribbean and elsewhere on England's south coast, so they were well versed in the level and detail of decision-making needed to create such a home. They had the confidence and experience to act as their own interior designers. They worked in close collaboration with their architects inside the house and with the well-known landscape designers, Colvin & Moggridge, in the creation of a sequence of garden spaces filled with planting robust enough to thrive in this maritime environment.

Nigel Anderson has over 30 years' experience in traditional and classical architecture and is well known for his new country houses and high quality housing schemes. He joined the Winchester-based ADAM Architecture in 1988 and became a director in 1991. He plays an important role in a broad spectrum of projects at the practice for both private clients and commercial developers, ranging from the restoration and refurbishment of historic houses to master planning at sites across the UK. He now has a wide variety of completed and in-progress projects across the country and the excellence of his new housing projects has been recognized by many local and national awards.

"With every completed project, I find it inspiring that what began with penciled sketches
on my drawing board, has escalated into an endeavor involving the interaction and collaboration
of always dozens, but sometimes hundreds, of people over months and years."

Nigel Anderson

ARROYO SECO
PASADENA, CALIFORNIA

Appleton & Associates

This modestly scaled, deceptively simple Italianate country villa fits both the Southern California region and its hillside site, offering the homeowner the perfect balance of simplicity and romance that they were seeking to achieve.

An exercise in master planning and structural engineering, the house is located on a small triangular lot perched on the edge of a precipitous slope. Yet with input from the owner, architect Marc Appleton was able to maximize every square inch of the property, while fully taking advantage of the spectacular and dramatic views of the oak-filled canyon below and mountains beyond.

Three stories in height, the house is slightly bowed in plan so that the main rooms open to a concave terrace, which embraces the principal view. This bowed plan also provides secondary views from each end of the house up and down the canyon. The southern, or convex, side of the house is anchored by a central stone stair and tower, with a loggia off the kitchen and family room leading to a small garden and lap pool. The footprint of the house is a compact 2,000 square feet.

The modestly finished interiors are decorated with an eclectic mix of California Plein Air paintings, family heirlooms, and new furniture pieces—including a dining room table and chairs by the late master furniture maker, Sam Maloof, an old friend of both the owner and architect.

Building materials were "of the earth" and included salvaged Italian terra cotta roof tiles, a rich rose stucco, old hand-hewn beams, and distressed wood plank floors. These finishes, along with careful craftsmanship and an eye to Mediterranean construction details, recreate the simple yet sophisticated feeling of an Italian hillside villa.

This award-winning firm was established by Marc Appleton in 1976, and has offices in Santa Monica and Santa Barbara, California. The firm specializes in the planning, design and landscaping of custom residential, institutional and commercial projects for both private and public clients. Projects include additions, restorations and the adaptive reuse of existing buildings as well as new construction. Marc is one of only eight designers who have been consistently named among *Architectural Digest's Top 100 Designers* since its inception in 1991.

"Although there are many players making up the game of architecture, our principal collaboration with our clients is the most important one. The best houses result from a process in which both parties are fully engaged."

Marc Appleton

A SUMMER RETREAT
CASHIERS, NORTH CAROLINA

James F. Carter Architect

Summer getaways to the cool Blue Ridge Mountains of North Carolina have been a Southern tradition for many years. Fond childhood memories were the initial draw to the area and the impetus for this project. The client expressed an appreciation for the numerous houses in the area that have passed down from generation to generation and the resulting sense of family history and tradition.

From the main road, one approaches the house by crossing a wooden bridge along a winding, gravel drive. Landscape Architect Stephen Lee Johnson of Sitework Studios worked to visually integrate the structure with its natural surroundings, using an abundance of native landscape plantings and thoughtfully positioned stone boulders. The house is sited near the crest of a hill but nestled into the mountain ridge, so as not to dominate the hilltop. Exterior materials of reclaimed wood, tree bark siding, and stone veneer pay respect to the regional vernacular and give the house an instant sense of belonging and permanence.

The genesis of the design – the idea of an old barn with a new purpose – is the large, two-story common room featuring an exposed timber-frame structure with plaster infill, south-facing bay window, and reclaimed wide plank flooring. Adjacent spaces are organized around the major east-west axis passing through this space. Room openings and windows on several cross axes offer multiple views of the distant mountains and flood the house with natural light. Changes in finished floor levels and varying ceiling heights maintain proper scale and proportion to increase the spatial experience.

Interior decorator Jane Hoke Bynum worked with the homeowner to procure appropriate furnishings, blending "fine" with the "not-so-fine," resulting in an understated, casual elegance.

James Carter opened his Birmingham, Alabama, design studio in 1996 after years of experience working with a respected local architect. The firm creates timeless homes that portray an "easy grace", where project concepts and designs are inspired by classical vernaculars, based on historical precedent that reflects the homeowner's lifestyle and personality. Highly detailed, hand-rendered construction drawings, along with James' personal involvement through project completion reflect the firm's hands-on philosophy. The firm's work can be seen throughout the Southeast and as far north as Massachusetts.

"For me, collaboration often goes hand in hand with inspiration. I enjoy working with talented people who bring their fresh ideas and experience to a project. I think the different perspectives help keep a designer's work fresh and constantly evolving."

James F. Carter

LONGWOOD FARM
CHAPPELL HILL, TEXAS

Curtis & Windham Architects

On the fringes of Texas Hill Country, a picturesque property of woodland, meadow, and creek immediately appealed to the clients, who sought to transform the former horse ranch into a family retreat and a place to entertain. Curtis & Windham set about creating a house that captures both the vernacular of the region and the spirit of an English park landscape. With this vision in mind, it followed that the design and placement of the house would be guided by an idealized relationship of the building to the site. A choreography of experiences, designed by Curtis & Windham's landscape architecture studio, explores these relationships.

Architecturally, the house presents a simple gabled mass with side wings that appear equal in size. A jogged plan shape and hierarchical massing follow the change in elevation and break down the volume as it uncoils around the front garden court. The principal mass of the house is clad in tumbled Texas Leuders limestone covered by a thin coat of parging, lending it a time-worn and permanent feel. Secondary wings are clad in wood siding, hinting at surrounding Hill Country farmhouses. The entire structure is unified with a coat of whitewash and a wood shake roof.

On the interior, a change in scale, proportion, and detail differentiates the hierarchy of spaces. Befitting its stature, the Great Room is the largest single volume and is distinguished by the use of a full Order. Detail in secondary rooms tends to the more simple expression of regional sources. The builder, R. B. Ratcliff & Associates, crafted custom moldings and millwork in-house that are complemented with a light neutral palette of paint and stains by the venerable Milam & Co. and plaster by Tobin & Rooney. The Great Room was deliberately aged with exposed joints and imperfections to give it a sense of history and to express reassurance that despite its architectural refinement, it is still a space for informal gathering. Furnishings selected by Ginger Barber reinforce the sense of welcoming and comfort with a nod to both vernacular and British themes.

A further image from this project can be found on page 6

Since the beginning of their collaboration in 1992, Bill Curtis and Russell Windham have found a mutual interest in producing traditional architecture that combines a deep respect for architectural history and context with a well-studied knowledge of traditional and classical detailing. Although best known for their work in Houston's historic suburbs, the firm has competed projects throughout the United States. Bill and Russell have both been recognized nationally in numerous publications, and are the recipients of numerous architectural awards.

*"Reaching across the allied arts of architecture, landscape architecture, and interior design
for an integrated approach inspires balance and unity in a project
that any single disciple on its own cannot easily achieve."*
Bill Curtis and Russell Windham

A FRENCH PROVINCIAL HOME
ATLANTA, GEORGIA

D. Stanley Dixon Architect

Sometimes adapting a house with a considerable history to the demands of modern family life requires reimagining it completely. But that doesn't necessarily mean the house has to lose its soul in the process—in fact, sometimes it can be regained. This home sits on a prominent site on one of the most elegant streets in Atlanta. Commissioned to replace the original 1930s house that was beyond repair, great care and consideration were given to designing a new home that stands at ease in its environment, while contributing to the dialog of a well-established street.

The exterior finishes are a harmonious blend of carved limestone, integrally colored stucco, a wood shake roof, and doors and windows meticulously detailed and built in Belgium. The result is a house that sits comfortably among its neighboring examples of eclectic Revival architecture from the 1920s to 1940s.

The plan is simple yet formal in its layout organized by an enfilade of rooms. The layout of the house was designed in a series of four pavilions made up of the main living area, the master, the garage, and the rear garden pavilion. Breaking the house into these distinct elements and connecting them by ancillary roofs and garden walls enables the size of the home to be disguised amongst this formal collection of structures.

The classical notion of *poche* is used throughout the house to create a sense of depth and definition to the interior spaces. The scale of the doors, windows, and ceiling heights vary throughout the home, in order to create a pleasing balance within the rooms, subtly defining the hierarchy of spaces. The interior was designed to be simple, restrained, and elegantly proportioned reflecting the character of French and Belgian interiors. There are also moments of surprise when subtle details are revealed.

Stan Dixon is an architect in Atlanta, Georgia specializing in traditional architecture with an understated elegance. His firm founded in 2005, has a passion for designing projects that are historically based in scale and proportion yet embrace the realization of modern living and welcomes the influence of modern design. His respect and awareness of context, combined with a focus on appropriateness of style, are essential design elements found throughout Stan's work. The firm is sensitive to historic precedent with an aesthetic and functionality that endures the test of time.

"We consider each project a unique opportunity for which we are committed to quality design and service to our clients. In the process of transcending our drawings into reality, we consider the collaboration of architect, client, builder, and consultants critical in creating one's home. Above all, "We work hard and love what we do!"

Stan Dixon

A GREEK REVIVAL TOWNHOUSE

SAVANNAH, GEORGIA

Franck & Lohsen Architects

In 2009, this 1850s Greek Revival townhouse was turned into a condo with the rear carriage house and the basement level split from the main house. Most of the home's original character was stripped, resulting in a bland and expected interior with virtually nothing done to the garden except for the addition of a pressure-treated deck.

Upon purchasing the property in 2012, the new owner, began working with Michael Franck of Franck & Lohsen Architects in Washington, DC, on an extensive restoration of the interior, in which period detailing was added, including a new Greek Revival column screen and two new Greek Revival mantlepieces. These new architectural elements recall the historic character of the original house through the use of Greek Revival detailing commensurate with the 1850s period. While the long-gone original detailing was much simpler, the owner and architect worked to create a more refined interior than would have been built originally. However, the detailing is of a scale and level of craftsmanship that honors the original house. The interior is tastefully and appropriately decorated by the owner with antique light fixtures, historic colors, modestly scaled furniture with updated fabrics all set amongst the owners' private collection of Grand Tour decorative pieces.

Immediately following the completion of the interior restoration, the new owner began work on the garden, which received a radical transformation. Working within the limitations of the 200-square-foot yard and maintaining the existing two-level terrace, the new garden design ensures enjoyment throughout the day and evening.

A further image from this project can be found on page 130.

As winners of the prestigious *Arthur Ross Award for Architecture* in 2011, Franck & Lohsen, Architects specialize in classical architecture and town planning. Founded by Michael M. Franck and Arthur C. Lohsen, their Washington, D.C., firm has earned distinction for its timeless and elegant designs, often with buildings or regions that are highly sensitive to their historic nature. With projects all over the United States as well as projects in Italy and in England, their work displays a thoughtful and sophisticated combination of classical approaches and modern sensibilities.

"On my quest to find the limitations which help inform the next decision, I find joy in teaming with someone who has taste, conviction, and the confidence of a restrained timeless aesthetic."

Michael Franck

A FEDERAL-STYLE RESIDENCE
HOUSTON, TEXAS

Allan Greenberg Architect

The beautiful River Oaks residential section of Houston, with its tree-lined streets and wide variety of traditional architecture, creates an ideal setting for a new house. It is a setting that inspires residents, because it is impeccably maintained, and architects, because it is a privilege and pleasure to create a new home here. The design challenge is threefold: to design a beautiful house, which is also a good neighbor to adjacent houses, and which pleases the client.

This house was designed for a family of five who enjoy entertaining. With open porches, front and rear, and large French doors throughout the first floor, the interior flows out easily to the exterior for parties. The main living-rooms all connect to one another through generous archways, providing guests with easy and continuous movement from room to room, and to the exterior.

The cornices in these rooms are similar in scale but have small differences in detail. The same is true of the ceiling decoration and mantles. Architectural elements like columns, entablatures, and architraves are painted a glossy white, but all the walls and ceilings have a matte finish. Room colors are soft and restricted to blue and white, plain white, or russet in the dining room, and an unusual shade of green in the kitchen. Floors throughout are a wide-plank French white oak with widths varying from 9 to 20 inches. The house was designed to display the owner's wonderful collection of American paintings, sculpture, and works on paper. The challenge was to provide the appropriate lighting level throughout to enhance works of varying size and character.

The previous house on the site also had a Mount Vernon-like portico. Architect Allan Greenberg chose to reuse this much-admired feature, believing that some sense of formal continuity was important to the neighborhood. The unusually large windows and tall French doors endow the mass of the house with a human scale. A glazed white arcade connects the house to the garage and was planned to define a small fenced garden.

A further image from this project can be found on page 1.

Allan Greenberg established his firm in 1972, and now has offices in Greenwich, New York, and Washington, D.C. The firm has an international reputation for combining contemporary construction techniques with the best architectural traditions to create solutions that are both timeless and technologically progressive. Allan's articles, teaching, and lectures have exerted a strong influence on the study and practice of classical architecture, and in 2006, he was the first American to be awarded the *Richard H. Driehaus Prize for Classical Architecture.*

*"A key part of an architect's job is working closely with your builder, subcontractors, and craftspeople.
Their collective ability to be creative, adding to the aesthetic intensity of the project,
can only occur in close collaboration with each other."*

Allan Greenberg

A MOUNTAIN HOME
WHITE SULPHUR SPRINGS, WEST VIRGINIA

Hamady Architects

This 15-acre site is located at the very tip of a mountain ridge, its land forming a semi conical shape with steep hills on three sides. The westerly approach from a private road straddling the ridge brings visitors to the end of the mountain, opening up to sweeping northern, easterly and southern vistas of valleys, fields and mountains. While the site offers dramatic and spectacular views, its topography and access presented challenges to the design for a large home with a vehicular forecourt, outdoor terraces and a garage.

In order to maintain harmonious relationships with the site and the surrounding landscape, architect Kahlil Hamady proposed design included carving the crest of the hill, embedding the house into it, crafting architectural forms that evoked the shapes of the hills and finally crowning the land with a humanly scaled and proportioned intervention. The composition was fundamentally sculptural in its intent, with respect to natural forms and the traditional order of architectural procession through public and private spaces. The most public space, the living room, was located in the center of the composition, bridging on a north-south axis a lawn terrace to the north overlooking a valley and a projecting porch, complete with flanking fireplaces, to the south that highlighted the relationship of the house with its surrounding landscape.

In addition to the evocation of natural forms, the house harbors architectural elements that are culturally meaningful to the owners, with the arched brackets stirring imagery of train stations, familiar to the legacies of the owners' family. Despite its topographical challenge, the house ultimately offers its owners a home that harmoniously weaves their cultural identity with the natural landscape.

While the house was being built, the superintendent, Peter Maraneck, a great craftsman, passed away. As a example of the important relationships that architects develop with the craftsmen who help them achieve their visions, Hamady Architects wish to honor the memory of Peter, in crediting this project to him.

Established in 1997 by Kahlil Hamady, the firm provides design services in the United States, Europe and Lebanon for residential urban and rural properties, assisting clients in developing comprehensive master plans informed by the inextricable relationship between architecture, landscape design and interior decoration. Kahlil's designs are rooted in a deep respect for nature and in each project's particular cultural context, along with historical and time-tested principles which inform and guide the design process. The Boston-based firm relies heavily on traditional methods of design including hand drawings, illustrations and paintings.

"Architecture is a creation of a culture. Its success is determined by the skills, talents, knowledge and genius of collaborating participants – patron, craftsman, designer and architect."

Kahlil Hamady

BLACK AND WHITE HOUSE
GREENWICH, CONNECTICUT

Ike Kligerman Barkley Architects

Completed in 2007 on a sloping site, the Black and White House is a residence that reacts to the landscape, reflects particular needs of modern family life, and creatively responds to the traditional tenets of 18th-century Swedish architecture. Ike Kligerman Barkley, led by architect Joel Barkley, began the project by looking to a country compound toured on a trip to Sweden: Linnaeus' Hammarby, the summer estate of Carolus Linnaeus and the scientist's family. The Linnaeus residence is composed of three buildings, each an edge to a central garden courtyard. Its pared down simplicity and graphic palette emphasized an elegance of proportion, representing a typically Nordic country seat.

With these ideals as design tenets, Barkley set to create a house that the clients, a young, growing family, could use as a primary residence. He designed an altered L-shape, which created both a courtyard effect when entering the property via car, as well as a striking profile for the formal front of the house, which opens out onto the family garden and sweeping lawn through the front door. The black and white palette emphasizes this distinction, and was decided early on in the design process. With the Linnaeus estate in mind, Barkley and the clients happened across an image of a black barn with white windows, also in the Swedish countryside. They decided to emulate this palette, emphasizing the striking graphic quality of the house's profile, with its peaked roof stretching 40 feet high. However, the palette was flipped on the courtyard side, creating a warm embrace of white stucco as one approaches the house.

Inside, the plan took a more contemporary turn: hallways were eliminated, and rooms flow from one to another. The entrance hall, with fireplace and main stair, acts as a cozy center of activity and movement. Boards were used throughout the interior, their detailing inspired by the interior of Linnaeus' Hammarby. The palette inside, selected in conjunction with interior designer Alexa Hampton, interprets the light-catching, sympathetic palettes of those Swedish country seats.

Further images from this project can be found on pages 38, 41, 42 and 43

Ike Kligerman Barkley, the New York and San Francisco based architecture and design firm, works throughout history and across styles always seeking to enhance life through good design. The firm produces residential environments as well as the occasional high profile public building. In their 25 years, the firm has designed buildings across the country and around the world, and has received numerous awards, including the *AIA New York Chapter Award*, the D&DB *Stars of Design Award*, and the *ICAA Julia Morgan Award*, as well as participating in the *Architectural Digest's* AD 100 since 1995.

*"A house is a rare opportunity for specific disciplines to flourish together.
The best designs are considered from inside-out and outside-in, with the "sister arts"
of interior design, architecture, and landscape architecture, to name but three."*

Joel Barkley

"People are often led astray to believe that classic details mean that the final result will be formulaic or generalized. This house was neither. It was different, personal, and filled with special moments."

Alexa Hampton

HOME FARM
YORKSHIRE ENGLAND

Francis Johnson and Partners

This new house at Hartforth follows in a rich Yorkshire tradition of Georgian designs by architects such as William Kent, James Paine, and John Carr. It replaces a simple early 19th-century stone farmhouse of no architectural merit on the same site, becoming the new principal structure on the estate. But unlike its undistinguished predecessor, this house, beautifully proportioned in local sandstone, is a noticeable eye-catcher within the estate's park landscape.

The new house is Janus-faced—inspired by a sketch by the late architect, Francis Johnson, completed in 1943 to wile away the time before being called up into the army during the Second World War. The north elevation, which faces onto the farmyard, is in a plain Palladian style whereas the south elevation, which faces onto the park, is in the Gothic style. The latter is justified by the fact that all the subsidiary farm buildings on the estate were cloaked in Gothic dress during the early 19th century.

This distinguished new house, designed by Digby Harris, draws heavily on historic precedent, with the compact plan based upon the popular 18th-century Georgian villas of architect Sir Robert Taylor. The Gothic façade features an elegant ogee window on one side looking out onto a small canal-type pond, with the main front boasting a full-height bow, bringing to mind older houses such as Corngreaves Hall in the West Midlands, with other elements taken from Batty Langley's seminal Gothic Architecture: Improved by Rules and Proportions, first published in 1747. The Palladian façade is dominated by a Diocletian window in the apex of the pediment, which provides the homeowner with an elevated platform from which to observe the comings and goings of the Hartforth Estate.

Chartered Architects Francis Johnson and Partners was founded in Yorkshire in 1937 by the late Francis F. Johnson, who was regarded as one of England's preeminent classical architects. The practice, now overseen by senior partners Digby Harris and Malcolm Stather, is best known for its Country House design – although they also design smaller houses and cottages, as well as commercial buildings, and interiors. The practice has received numerous awards over the years including, most recently, the 2009 Giles Worsley Award for a *New Building in a Georgian Context* from the Georgian Group.

"It is rare for client and architect to be completely in accord but, when it does happen,
it makes for the happiest of jobs and a house of which both can be equally proud."

Digby Harris

A CLASSICAL TOWNHOUSE
CHICAGO, ILLINOIS

Liederbach & Graham Architects

This property is located in Lincoln Park, a neighborhood of Chicago that is well known for its eclectic architectural fabric. Architects Liederbach & Graham responded to this context by contributing a home that is intended to offer the quiet repose of a Georgian house that one might find along London's more fashionable streets and squares. The relatively austere expression of Georgian architecture is interrupted only by the elegant, Lutyens-inspired entrance with an exuberantly broken pediment. Two wrought iron arms gently hold an English lantern above the steps and illuminate the fanlight inspired by a similar design from the late 18th-century architect Robert Adam.

The rusticated limestone base and entry are made of heroically sized pieces of limestone. The second and third floors are constructed of handmade Tuscan red waterstruck brick, laid in a Flemish bond pattern with black headers. Each brick was specifically drawn to ensure the pattern was seamless and not a single brick had to be cut. Humble Chicago common brick was reclaimed and used on the home's other elevations, rendering them with an instant patina and a connection to the original homes of the neighborhood and the city at large.

The clients wanted the private realm of the home's interior to be emblematic of their more adventurous side. Central to this is the pairing of architects Liederbach & Graham and acclaimed interior decorator Steven Gambrel. Blending a robust yet highly detailed interior classical architecture with an extraordinary sense of color, detail, and interior decoration, the results are almost like a hip young couple has moved into an 18th-century London townhouse. Throughout the home, the rooms are meticulously proportioned, and precisely planned and tailored to avoid feeling too large. This sense of both intimacy and importance is achieved by carefully combining generous ceiling heights with a contemporary take on Georgian-inspired details, such as the staircase, plaster moldings, wood paneling, and wainscoting.

Further images from this project can be found on pages 23, 44, 47, 48 and 49.

Friends since graduate school, R. Michael Graham and Phillip J. Liederbach founded Liederbach & Graham Architects in 1991 to pursue their long held interest in traditional, vernacular and classical domestic architecture. The partners share a passion for the close study of historical precedent and the application of this connoisseurship upon new and relevant architecture. Phillip and Michael have kept their Chicago-based design studio intentionally small, creating an atmosphere conducive to a thoughtful collaboration between the clients, interior designers, landscape architects and craftsman which is essential to creating work that will endure.

"The chemistry of a great collaboration is contagious. It's wonderful to watch all of the tradespeople pursue excellence with the same vigor and sense of purpose."

Phillip Liederbach

"As the rooms are carefully furnished and styled with objects to reinforce the color palette and characteristics of the space, they take on a life of their own, and ultimately appear to have been there for generations, only adapted and refreshed along the way."

Steven Gambrel

ON POINT FARM
CHESTER COUNTY, PENNSYLVANIA

John Milner Architects

This new residence and complex of farm and equestrian structures buildings were designed with respect for the vernacular architectural traditions of the region. Historically, the majority of those who settled in this area were of English ancestry, and farmed the land to produce crops, raise livestock, and process the materials that supported their lives.

Having grown up in this environment, the clients shared a great appreciation for the simple and well-proportioned fieldstone buildings that had incrementally evolved within the landscape as the settlers became more prosperous and their families expanded. With this in mind, architect John Milner was engaged to design the house and outbuildings to reflect these qualities and to fit naturally into the topography of a large and environmentally sensitive area of conserved open space, while also providing a contemporary and functional living and working environment.

As a transition between the vastness of the agrarian landscape and the more structured composition of the house, an entrance garden on the south (front) side was created and defined by a high fieldstone wall. The rugged texture and graceful curves of the wall are juxtaposed with the more refined stonework and right-angled façades of the house. The enclosed space affords an intimate and private domestic precinct through which both family and guests pass as part of the entry sequence. The floor plan arrangement provides opportunities for a variety of sequential vistas through the house and onto the farmland beyond. Many of the rooms feature wood paneling and related millwork, salvaged from an historic late-18th-century house that had been demolished nearby. New woodwork was designed to complement the authentic materials, and antique random-width yellow pine flooring was installed throughout. Handcrafted wrought iron hinges and locks, both antique and reproduction, were installed on doors and cabinetry.

Further images from this project can be found on pages 111 and 113.

John Milner Architects specializes in the evaluation, restoration and adaptation of historic buildings, as well as the design of new homes which reflect the rich architectural traditions of the past. The firm's firsthand experience with the history and construction technology of three centuries of American architecture informs its approach to both historic preservation and new design. The firm, located in Chadds Ford, Pennsylvania, is led by principals Christopher Miller, Mary Werner DeNadai, and John Milner has been responsible for directing and implementing numerous new design and preservation projects recognized for their excellence on local and national levels.

"*Design is the first step, but craftsmen's contributions are key to realizing, enriching, and giving personality to a final creation.*"

John Milner

A NEW FARMHOUSE
COLUMBIA COUNTY, NEW YORK

John B. Murray Architect

Located on a 120-acre parcel of upstate New York farmland, with beautiful views of the Berkshires to the north, architect John Murray was commissioned to design a new 6,700-square-foot farmhouse that would feel timeless—as if it had always been there—yet livable, functional, and sustainable for today's modern living.

The design of this home is based upon the concept of vernacular progression—the manner in which a house grows and evolves over time. This fictional narrative started with a modest fieldstone cottage, built by an 18th-century Dutch farmer. As the family prospered, a stately Federal farmhouse was attached, and in the keeping of New England farm buildings, the family later added a "little house" and a "back house" for the kitchen, mudroom, and family room. At some point during this fictional narrative a barn was also constructed.

Period-specific building materials, finishes, and architectural elements further enhance the historical illusion. The Federal-style main house welcomes more refined details, with plaster cornices, entablatures above the windows, painted paneled walls, and a lead-coated copper roof. The old Dutch wing has rustically finished parged walls, hewn ceiling beams, wood shutters and a cedar shake roof. The final additions take on a scaled-back Shaker style with stained and glazed cabinetry against reclaimed lumber walls and a flush board ceiling. Interior designer Sam Blount decorated the entire house.

A 19th-century barn—complete with hand-hewn timbers—was found in Buffalo, New York, disassembled, repaired, and painstakingly rebuilt on this property. It now serves as the homeowner's workshop. A two-car garage was discretely added as a lean-to structure.

A further image from this project can be found on page 27.

For over 15 years John Murray's New York City office has been lauded for its traditional aesthetic, its simplicity of form, and in particular, its supreme craftsmanship. Starting with hand-drawn plans, the firms design's all reflect their context, while seamlessly integrating sophisticated and unique details. This old world care, and respect for the creative clarity that comes from a visual as well as in-person dialogue between client and architect, are the firm's hallmark. Over the years John has collaborated with many of America's top decorators, as is considered an expert on the Park Avenue vernacular.

"Collaboration allows us the opportunity to realize the exceptional quality of design work that we strive to achieve. As an architect, I work together with the finest design professionals and artisans in a variety disciplines to create beautiful spaces for living."

John B. Murray

BOXWOOD
NASHVILLE, TENNESSEE

G. P. Schafer Architect

Sometimes adapting a house with a lot of history to the demands of modern family life requires completely reimagining it. But that doesn't necessarily mean it has to lose its soul in the process—sometimes it actually regains it. This 14,000-square-foot Charles Platt-designed house in the Belle Meade suburb of Nashville was originally built in 1914. It was then substantially altered in the 1950s with the re-cladding of its façade in brick, the complete reconfiguring of its interior, and the addition of an entry portico, garages, and outbuildings. Altered again in the 1990s, much of the charm of Platt's original design had been lost by 2005, when our clients bought the house.

Believing in the validity of Platt's original vision, we completely reworked the house once again, in order to restore the substance of his original interior, reintroduce the original French doors out to the garden, and rebuild the 1950s portico in a manner more suited to Platt's architecture. Most importantly, we adapted the house to the 21st-century lifestyle of a young family with three small children, whose lives revolve around a large new kitchen, family and informal dining rooms.

Working in close collaboration with Nashville landscape architect Gavin Duke and the interior decorator David Netto over four years, our design has allowed the house to regain the classical elegance and understated formality of its original form, while at the same time achieving a livability, freshness, and vitality through the modern traditionalism of the interior architectural detailing and decoration. All this was accomplished while remaining within the footprint of the original house, as mandated by the local zoning board.

Further images from this project can be found on pages 22, 24 and 246.

G. P. Schafer Architect is a New York City-based firm specializing in classical and traditional residential architecture. In each of its projects the firm emphasizes a commitment to quality, craftsmanship, rigorous detail based on an understanding of historic precedent and, most importantly, comfort and livability. Led by principal Gil Schafer III, the firm has been widely published in books and periodicals on both sides of the Atlantic and has been the recipient of numerous awards including three Palladio Awards for outstanding traditional residential design.

"To make a house that is truly beautiful, comfortable, and feels connected with the land, requires that architects, landscape designers, and decorators engage in a dialogue with each other from the start of a project to its finish. To create something in which you can no longer discern where one person's contribution ends and the other's begins."

Gil Schafer

A CLASSICAL REVIVAL TOWNHOUSE
SAN FRANCISCO, CALIFORNIA

Andrew Skurman Architects

This new townhouse is located in the Pacific Heights area of San Francisco, on a block where the front of the house faces a park to the south, while the rear overlooks the San Francisco Bay to the north. The area is well known for its amalgamation of architectural styles—ranging from classical to contemporary—and engaging in this dialog was one of the main design objectives of architect Andrew Skurman.

Drawing upon his time as a student at Cooper Union in New York City, Skurman was inspired by the historic La-Grange Terrace, and in particular its monumental portico, which is elevated one story above the hustle and bustle of Lafayette Street below. Using those same principles, Skurman chose to pull forward the garage of this townhouse, creating a plinth, which would support the two-story Doric columns of a newly created outdoor terrace. The scale of the columns also provides a powerful street presence, which allows this relatively small building to have a great conversation with the two abutting structures. But rather than adding a typical solid roof to provide shade, Skurman and his team opted for an open pergola which, instead, would allow sunlight into all of the rooms facing the portico. Elevated above the street, the terrace not only provides magnificent views of Alta Plaza, it also facilitates the indoor/outdoor lifestyle of northern California.

Located in the center of the townhouse is an elegant staircase, which spirals up through three floors and is lit from above by a circular skylight. The stair hall also serves as the central organizing feature from which all the major spaces are accessed. Working with classically detailed interiors, designer Martha Angus decorated the rooms with more contemporary furnishings and carefully selected artwork. And with open-concept planning a premium for modern-day living, the family room and kitchen are designed as a single space, which opens out onto the terrace beyond.

A further image from this project can be found on page 25.

Andrew Skurman founded his firm in 1992 in San Francisco. As principal and owner of Andrew Skurman Architects, he focuses on superbly crafted custom houses that are perfectly and logically planned to the specific requirements and wishes of his clients. His expertise lies in the elegant and refined expression of classical architecture and the interpretation of French, Georgian, and Mediterranean styles. Andrew has received the honor of being named a Chevalier of Arts & Letters by the Minister of Culture of France.

"The most important relationship is the one between the client and the architect. The collaboration begins the very moment we sit down and I am granted the opportunity to listen to the client's desires and program. Then with the use of a blank piece of paper and a pencil we work on the initial concepts and design."

Andrew Skurman

PALLADIAN VILLA
WILTSHIRE, ENGLAND

George Saumerez Smith, ADAM Architecture

Sitting on the edge of a small hamlet in rural Wiltshire, on the site of a redundant dairy farm, this new house is firmly in the spirit of Italian Renaissance architect Andrea Palladio's villa-farms. The house reflects the owners' passion for Italy, as well as their bold taste in interior decoration and gardening. The entrance front is relatively simple and understated, the three central bays forming an arcade as an enclosed entrance portico or loggia. By contrast, the garden front is more architectural, with a central Doric portico closely following the Order illustrated in Palladio's treatise, *I Quattro Libri dell'Architettura*.

The plan developed from the idea that the house might originally have been built by intrepid travellers bringing their ideas back to England from Italy. The loggia was originally built as a completely open arcade, with the front door set well back in a sheltered position. Over time, the owners realized that such an arrangement would suit the Italian climate better than the English, and so they glazed in the loggia and, at the same time, they added a service wing. While this fictitious history might appear whimsical, it gives the house logic and an added layer of interest so that, for example, the glazed doors of the loggia are different from those on the rest of the house.

The house is built in natural stone and lime render with a slate roof, and an attached service wing built in red brick. Natural materials are also widely used throughout the interior of the house, including the main staircase, which is entirely built in Portland stone. The central part of the house is decorated in muted soft colours, with bold sculptural panels designed and made in stucco by architectural sculptor Geoffrey Preston.

From a site that was covered in concrete and tarmac until five years ago, the garden has become quickly established. As with any new house, it needs mature trees nearby to feel properly at home and, as time goes on, the house will increasingly become a natural part of the landscape.

George Saumarez Smith, a Director at the Winchester-based ADAM Architecture, is one of the UK's leading young classical architects. His work includes both new buildings and alterations, extensions and repairs to historic properties and he has also been involved in design consultancy and urban master-planning on several projects. George is passionate about measuring and drawing historic buildings and his work has been exhibited and published widely, both in the UK and abroad. He has received various awards for his work and was one of six shortlisted architects for the RIBA's 2011 *Young Architect of the Year Award*.

DETAIL · OF · THE · EAST · FACADE
OF THE NEW HOUSE AT WEDHAMPTON · WILTS
COMPLETED IN 2009   ONE METRE   GEORGE SAUMAREZ SMITH · ARCH.T

DETAIL · OF · THE · WEST · FACADE
OF THE NEW HOUSE AT WEDHAMPTON · WILTS
COMPLETED IN 2009   HALF A METRE   GEORGE SAUMAREZ SMITH · ARCH.T

*"Architectural training seems to encourage everyone to work as individuals.
You discover later that being a good architect is really about how you collaborate with others."*

George Saumerez Smith

LA CHOSA
PALM BEACH FLORIDA

Smith Architectural Group

Situated in the heart of Palm Beach, La Chosa is a landmark Mediterranean home that was originally built in 1923 by the noted Palm Beach architect Marion Sims Wyeth. Working with an experienced design team, this historic property was given a more updated look while still honoring its storied past.

The current owners of the home were interested in preserving the public areas while updating the rest of the house to accommodate their lifestyle. Their large family required more bedrooms and areas for socializing. The organization of rooms around the courtyard remained: the dining room, living room, and foyer along with the loggias, frame the courtyard space but the old west wing of the house, which accommodated a warren of staff rooms and ancillary spaces, was removed. The large new addition allowed for a breakfast room, family room, family loggia, and expanded kitchen, as well as four additional bedrooms and a sitting area.

Landscape architect Mario Nievera reclaimed the rear of the property by unifying it into an expansive lawn area. The 1960s guesthouse, which awkwardly "kissed" the historic structure was replaced with a new guesthouse, which sits at the east end of the north lawn and is centered on the swimming pool. At the west side of the lawn is the new family loggia and family room beyond. The design team took advantage of the new loggia, as well as the restored courtyard and pool area, to create multiple vignettes for relaxing outdoors. This relationship between the architecture, interior design, and landscape design is especially important in a tropical environment, as the exterior living spaces are enjoyed as much as the interiors, and the line between what is inside and outside becomes blurred. Interior designer Sherrill Canet used the garden views and beautiful light as an inspiration for the interior color palette. The exterior spaces are as well-appointed as the interiors and flow seamlessly together, ensuring that this historic home will be cherished for generations to come.

Since opening his office in 1989, Jeffrey Smith has established a practice that is committed to the pursuit of classical architecture. Following in the tradition of Palm Beach's celebrated architects of the past, Jeff's work displays a refined elegance coupled with exquisite detailing and superb craftsmanship. He subscribes to the idiom that the rebirth of tradition yields architecture with meaning. Much respected in Palm Beach, he has served as Chairman of the Town's Architectural Commission and Landmark Preservation Commission.

*"I believe that when the architect, interior designer, and landscape architect collaborate it creates
a synergy that results in a combined effect greater than the sum of their separate roles."*

Jeff Smith

CREOLE COLONIAL
NEW ORLEANS, LOUISIANA

Ken Tate Architect

Gumbo—a quintessential New Orleans recipe marrying French, Spanish, and Native American influences—is a perfect metaphor to describe the mélange of cultures found within this house. At first glance, the façade's hipped roof and deep porch resemble Louisiana French plantation architecture—a likeness reinforced by the porch's stucco-over-brick columns, brick floor, and painted ceiling beams. Situated on a spit of land surrounded by canals, the house also invites comparison to the island plantations of the French West Indies. Like these compounds, this property includes a central dwelling surrounded by attached and detached outbuildings, strung together like pearls on a string.

However, unlike the French doors common in Creole architecture, this house employs double-hung windows and a delicate front door surround with fluted pilasters and a fanlight. Tate chose these elements to invoke the Federal architecture of New Orleans' late 18th and early 19th-century American neighborhoods. Working alongside Ann Holden of Holden and Dupuy Interiors, the home is decorated to reflect local history and culture—best highlighted in the dining room, where Gracie & Company mural wallpaper depicts steaming swamp waters, knobby cypress trees and Spanish moss, creating the illusion that one has stepped into the pre-colonial Louisiana landscape.

The living room, with cavernous proportions, massive painted ceiling beams, and large arched windows was inspired by the bold majesty of the Spanish Cabildo's official chamber. "I imagined this room feeling like a grand entertaining space in a colonial governor's house," says Tate. Yet here, as elsewhere in the house, cultural and stylistic expressions intersect. Beneath the room's Spanish arches, Federal fanlights crown French doors, serving as more reminders of New Orleans' gumbo soul.

A further image from this project can be found on pages 14 and 15.

New Orleans architect Ken Tate started his eponymous firm in 1984, and since then has become one of the most sought after designers in the United States. Ken's understanding of classical architecture is enhanced by his love of vernacular styles, and while some of his designs offer a faithful representation of historic styles, others marry elements from several periods to give the impression that they grew and changed over time. By employing this design technique, as well as the use of traditional craftsmanship, all of his homes have a romantic feel that makes them appear to have been lived in for generations. The firms work has been published extensively with his last book *A Classical Journey: The House of Ken Tate* becoming an instant best-seller.

"When a client comes to an architect, they are usually following a dream.
The architect's job is to dream their house into existence, pulling it into three-dimensional
reality through a process of experiential imagining."

Ken Tate

NEWHAM

CORNWALL ENGLAND

Russell Taylor Architects

England is a land rich in building materials. How these materials are used and how buildings respond to the landscape creates the distinct character of each and every region. But this pattern of building, using local materials to create a sense of identity, is slowly being destroyed by a desire to break with the past and our rich traditions. To be different, for the sake of being different—and even worse, to merely seek attention—nowadays, many new homes are created in a could-be-anywhere landscape, devoid of any cultural meaning or significance. Newham resists this decline by using local materials—granite, slate, and rubblestone—and through building in a distinctively Cornish way. It is a classical house, that is to say it is designed following principles, which have dominated architecture since antiquity. Classicism favors good proportions, simple shapes, and carefully considered ornament.

The home commands a stunning view of the Fowey River, and is designed to be worthy of its site. It is long and low with all the principal rooms facing the view down the river. The main entrance is approached from the land side and is marked by massive granite gate piers, beyond these is the entrance portico of four monolithic Greek Doric columns. There is a pleasing parallel: the Classical worlds of Greece and Rome favored monoliths, while Cornwall has always favored them because granite is so hard to work.

Inside, simplicity is the keynote, but on a generous scale. The rough-hewn quality of the exterior is moderated but it remains very much a house of the country. For the interiors, there was no suitable Cornish stone available and so Portland stone varieties with lots of shell and fossils were selected. The columns forming the screen in the double-height entrance hall are, like those in the portico, Doric, but here a more refined, slender Doric. The columns are also monoliths and display an intriguing history of marine sedimentation from top to bottom.

Russell Taylor specializes in the contemporary application of classical principles with work encompassing new buildings, conservation, interiors and furniture design. The ethos of his award winning practice, which has offices in Cornwall and London, is to design beautiful timeless architecture: sustainable, practical and cost effective. In addition to designing houses for private clients he also undertakes ecclesiastical and public sector work. Russell Taylor is a powerful advocate for the promotion of classical design. He is active in supporting those with similar aims and is an executive committee member of the Georgian Group.

"The art of architecture grows out of fruitful collaboration – it cannot be made without the varied building crafts working together with architect and client."

Russell Taylor

KINGSHAM FARM

SUSSEX, ENGLAND

Quinlan and Francis Terry Architects

Kingsham Farm is a medium-sized classical house recently completed near Liphook in Sussex. It consists of five bays with a portico over the central three windows. The walls are constructed from random Sussex sandstone with a roof of irregular stone slates.

The plan is centred on a hall that spans the full depth of the house with a staircase and main rooms leading off it. This hall is for circulation and a room in its own right with a generous Palladian fireplace as a focus. Ionic pilasters give the hall structure, which is carried through to the coffers on the ceiling.

The most unusual feature of the house is the elaborate Baroque door surround, which contrasts with the simplicity of the rest of the design. Inspirations for this door surround are East European architectural examples, most notably St. Nicholas Church in Prague, designed by Christoph Dientzenhofer. In common with many Czech examples, the spayed jambs are twisted to give the entrance a dramatic effect. This is further heightened by the giant shell over the door. The use of architectural motifs from anywhere other than Italy and France is rare in English classical architecture, which makes this doorcase all the more unusual.

Kingsham Farm has a summerhouse in the grounds, which is designed around a simple Palladian Doric portico. This has a practical application as a place to sit out overlooking the pool.

A further image from this project can be found on pages 2 and 3.

Together with his father Quinlan Terry, Francis Terry operates one of the most celebrated and influential architectural firms practicing today. As leading proponents in the revival of classical architecture, their firm emphasizes traditional materials, construction methods, and ornament as a valuable solution to modern architecture. Their firm located in the small Essex village of Dedham, continues the architectural practice that was started in 1928 by the late Raymond Erith, specializing in Palladian inspired designs. Both Quinlan and Francis have been honored with numerous awards, including the *Richard H. Driehaus Prize for Classical Architecture.*

"Architecture paints on a far broader canvas, which requires the collaboration of many differently skilled people in its execution – and this is, in essence, the joy of architecture."

Francis Terry

ROSEBROOK

NEW CANAAN, CONNECTICUT

Wadia Associates

This Elizabethan manor house is perched on a hill, taking in the sweeping views of the surrounding New England landscape. Intertwining Gothic and Renaissance elements that together yield something entirely of its own, Wadia Associates decided early on that the Elizabethan style was the perfect vehicle for maximizing these spectacular views while also meeting the planning needs of the homeowners.

The asymmetrical plan arrangement, combined with an abundance of natural light, make the design a perfect fit for today's modern family. Although each of the principal rooms are designed as "garden rooms," each is treated differently, due to the many variations of windows and also the diverse planting schemes employed around the perimeter of the building. The dining room provides views of a manicured rose garden; the living room opens onto an entertaining terrace; the stair hall opens to a covered loggia; and the kitchen overlooks a seasonal herb garden. A conservatory sits at the end of the house, providing the homeowner with panoramic views of the property and the ever-changing foliage of the New England countryside beyond.

The windows, set off by stone mullions, half timbering, gable ends, high chimneys, steeply pitched slate roofs, finials, and whimsical ogee arches, all combine to create the Elizabethan aesthetic.

Decorative rosette motifs are incorporated throughout, knitting together the exterior and interior of the home. Inside, although more contemporary in its appearance, the home includes traditional bespoke details such as a mahogany paneled library, a limestone fireplace carved by Traditional Cut Stone Ltd., and an oil-rubbed bronze balustrade—forged locally in Connecticut. This attention to detail is what successfully fuses together the architecture with the interiors and the garden. It also gives the impression that the home is far older than it actually is.

For over thirty years, Dinyar Wadia has earned a reputation for designing classically inspired homes, gardens and interiors in New Canaan, Connecticut. His finely detailed residences display a remarkable versatility and adaptability within the classical language, and are characterized by a passion for excellent detailing, use of fine materials and exceptional workmanship. Dinyar's core design philosophy is to emphasize the integral relationship between a home and its gardens – an approach that has seen him garner numerous architectural and landscape design awards.

"Collaboration with the other disciplines only ends when Mother Nature takes the helm."

James Doyle and Kathyrn Herman

"The most successful projects occur when everyone performs in harmony. The architect may well be the conductor, and the client the patron, but it is the builders and craftsmen that form the orchestra — with the interior designer being the featured violinist."

Dinyar Wadia

A FRENCH COUNTRY HOUSE
BRYN MAWR, PENNSYLVANIA

Peter Zimmerman Architects

The design objectives for this French country house, on Philadelphia's Main Line, were to seamlessly blend a house with the landscape, while remaining true to the architectural detail and materials appropriate for a house of this era.

The interior layout was designed to create a visual separation of formal and informal spaces. The spaces necessary to accommodate more formal entertaining are oriented along the front of the house and accessed directly off the formal courtyard and entrance foyer. The informal spaces, dedicated to the day-to-day functions of the family, are located along the rear of the house. They extend out to the gardens and terraces, creating a sense of transparency and integration with the landscape. The orientation of the kitchen, family room, family dining, and garden room allow the family to enjoy natural light and the beautiful landscape on a daily basis. The elongation of the site axis terminates at the pool gazebo, which is nestled between two mature trees and completes the view from the main garden room terrace.

Simple but not simplistic, traditional building materials enhance the richness of the design while also subtly creating a hierarchy of design. The stucco is a natural blend of sand and stone, with cracks intentionally left to create the illusion of age. The formal front of the house features limestone window surrounds, while the informal areas have limestone sills with wood surrounds. A wood cedar roof and custom hand-forged ironwork, as well as copper gutters and downspouts all seamlessly blend into the whole—with the latter used as a vertical element to balance the horizontal volumes of the house.

Peter Zimmerman founded his firm in 1982 as a full service residential design firm located on Philadelphia's Main Line. Peter has produced an extensive portfolio of award winning private residences, equestrian centers and private wineries across the country. The firms design philosophy is deeply rooted in the historic traditions of architecture: classical proportion and scale, the balance of shadow and light, and the importance of the sustainable relationship between materials. Their designs focus on the seamless integration between the built and natural environment.

"Our design process is the expression of the dialog between client and architect; a willingness to explore possibilities with the realization that there is never a single answer or solution."
Peter Zimmerman

CREDITS

About the Author

"I can't tell you what pride and joy it gives me to see what my alumni are up to. Your example makes it even more imperative that we can continue to produce more practitioners like yourself for the future."
– H.R.H. The Prince of Wales

A native of Manchester, England, Phillip attended the prestigious Prince of Wales' Institute of Architecture in London. He received a Degree in Architecture from his hometown university, before moving to America, where he gained a Masters in Architecture from The University of Notre Dame.

After training with some of the most recognized residential architectural firms in America, Phillip started his own design firm *Phillip James Dodd: Bespoke Residential Design*. With a reputation as one of the foremost experts on classical architecture and interiors, Phillip is fast becoming one of the most sought-after young residential designers practicing today. His designs can be found in Manhattan, Greenwich, and Palm Beach—ranging from an 800-square-foot (74-square-meter) pied-à-terre to a 20,000-square-foot (1,858-square-meter) waterfront estate property.

He is a Fellow Emeritus at the Institute of Classical Architecture and Art and, most recently, was unanimously elected by his peers to become a member of the exclusive INTBAU College of Traditional Practitioners—a peak international professional body for practitioners in traditional buildings arts, architecture, and urbanism. He has lectured extensively throughout the United States on the subject of classical architecture.

Phillip is the author of the highly acclaimed *The Art of Classical Details: Theory Design and Craftsmanship*, and is a regular contributor to *VENÜ Magazine*. He is also the author of *New Classicists: Wadia Associates*, which features a foreword by H.R.H. The Prince of Wales. Currently, he is working with photographer Jonathan Wallen on a lavish new volume on *The Beaux-Art Architecture of New York City*, featuring a foreword by S. Christopher Meigher III.

ABOVE:
The author, Phillip James Dodd, photographed inside a recently completed Georgian style home in Greenwich, Connecticut.

OPPOSITE:
Design drawings for a new Anglo-Caribbean style home in Palm Beach, Florida, along with a copy of *The Art of Classical Details: Theory, Design and Craftsmanship. Phillip James Dodd*

Acknowledgements

When I first started my architectural education, my grandmother gave me a stipend to purchase one architecture book a month. Many years later this has become a habit—or one could argue, an addiction—that I have maintained. As an undergraduate though, these books allowed me to discover what was not being taught in the classroom—namely the resurgence of classical design. These books became my inspiration and helped shape my career. Two of my earliest purchases were monographs published in the early 1990s by Academy Editions on the works of architects Quinlan Terry and Allan Greenberg. And so it is especially humbling to have these two pallbearers of modern-day classicism featured in the pages of my own book. My hope is that their work, along with the work of everyone else featured in this book, will inspire others just as they have inspired me.

In the words of Ellie Cullman, "This wonderful new book addresses the fundamental issue of collaboration between architect, decorator, landscaper, and the enormous cast of characters who bring their formidable talents to the realization of every project." Well, just like the subject matter in these pages, this volume is a collaborative effort, and I am indebted to all those who have shared their talents—writers, designers, photographers, and artists alike. I am especially grateful to those behind the scenes, working in the offices of the featured architects, who helped to collate and submit all of the material that you see here*.

As with the first volume, it is especially gratifying to be able to feature the work of many people with whom I have become friends over the years—as well as people who I have had the privilege of working alongside. For a short period of time in the late 1990s the New York firm of Fairfax & Sammons Architects attracted a remarkable group of designers. I am proud to be part of this talented alumni and I am honored to be able to feature the work and writing of past colleagues William Bates, Michael Franck, and Ben Pentreath. Although not featured in these pages, I would also like to acknowledge Richard Dragasic, Robert Morris, William Oster, Stephen Piersanti, Seth Joseph Weine, and Richard Sammons—from whom I collectively learnt many of the principals that are shared in this book.

With one eye on the past and one firmly on the future, I'd like to thank all of those with whom I have had the great honor of collaborating with and learning from—as well as expressing my eagerness for what the future has in store. In particular I would like to thank Saranda Berisa, Hossien Kazemi, Christopher Meigher, Lynn Scalo, Ken Tate, Tracey Thomas, and Jonathan Wallen for their support and friendship.

I would also like to thank everyone at Images Publishing Group especially Paul Latham and Rod Gilbert for their patience and skill in putting this book together. This is our second book together, and I look forward to being part of the IMAGES family for many years to come.

My final thanks are reserved for my family, as they continue to be the source of my inspiration. I could not have asked for a more supportive and loving family—and it is for this in life that I am most grateful. To my parents, brother, and my dearest Theresa, I love you.

* Special thanks to Annatina Aaronson, author of the text featured on page 147.

BOXWOOD (see page 197): A view into the new oak paneled library, and living room beyond, of this remodeled house originally designed by the great American classicist Charles A. Platt in 1915.

G. P. Schafer Architect

Library

Ever since starting my architectural education I have developed the habit – or should I say addiction – of acquiring a book every month. What started off as a few books on those architects I wished to emulate has now blossomed into a collection of close to 1,000 volumes on architecture, interior design, landscape design, and the allied arts. After all, one of the bonuses of the collaborative process is that you not only work alongside other design professionals, you also have an opportunity to learn from them.

Below is a list of 20 of my most recent book purchases – many authored by those featured in these pages. By no means an exhaustive list, these are volumes that I often reference for inspiration.

Architecture

**The Art of Classical Details:
Theory, Design and Craftsmanship**
Phillip James Dodd
Images Publishing Group, 2013
ISBN: 978-186470233

The New Shingled House
Ike Kligerman Barkley
The Monacelli Press, 2015
ISBN: 978-1580934435

**Classical Invention: The Architecture
of John B. Murray**
John B. Murray
The Monacelli Press, 2013
ISBN: 978-1580933681

A Treatise on Modern Architecture in Five Books
George Saumarez Smith
The Bardwell Press, 2013
ISBN: 978-1905622504

A Classical Journey: The Houses of Ken Tate
Ken Tate
Images Publishing Group, 2011
ISBN: 978-1864702903

Interior Design and Decoration

Mario Buatta: Fifty Years of American Interior Design
Mario Buatta
Rizzoli, 2013
ISBN: 978-0847840724

**The Detailed Interior: Decorating Up Close
with Cullman & Kravis**
Elissa Cullman and Tracey Pruzan
The Monacelli Press, 2013
ISBN: 978-1580933551

Time and Place
Steven Gambrel
Abrams, 2012
ISBN: 978-1419700682

Decorating in Detail
Alexa Hampton
Potter Style, 2013
ISBN: 978-0307956859

**English Decoration: Timeless Inspiration
for the Contemporary Home**
Ben Pentreath
Ryland Peters & Small, 2012
ISBN: 978-1849752664

Landscape Design

**The Landscape Designs of Doyle Herman
Design Associates**
James Doyle and Kathyrn Herman
Images Publishing Group, 2013
ISBN: 978-1864705034

Le jardin Plume
Gilles Le Sacnff-Mayer
Les Editions Eugen Ulmer (French), 2008
ISBN: 978-2841383399

Forever Green
Mario Nievera
Pointed Leaf Press, 2012
ISBN: 978-0983388999

The New English Garden
Tim Richardson
Frances Lincoln, 2013
ISBN: 978-0711232709

Historic Precedent

**The Art of CFA Voysey: English Pioneer,
Modernist Architect and Designer**
David Cole
Images Publishing Group, 2014
ISBN: 978-1864706048

**The Drawing Room: English Country
House Decoration**
Jeremy Musson and Paul Barker
Rizzoli, 2014
ISBN: 978-0847843336

**New York Transformed:
The Architecture of Cross & Cross**
Peter Pennoyer and Anne Walker
The Monacelli Press, 2014
ISBN: 978-1580933803

The Buildings and Designs of Andrea Palladio
Ottavio Berotti Scamozzi
(Classic Reprint Series)
Princeton Architectural Press, 2014
ISBN: 978-1616892647

Specialty Design

Color: Natural Palettes for Painted Rooms
Donald Kaufman and Taffy Dahl
Clarkson Potter, 1992
ISBN: 978-0517576601

Carl Laubin: Paintings
John Russell Taylor and David Watkin
Philip Wilson Publishers, 2007
ISBN: 978-0856676338

Effortless and elegant, this new house evokes the work of
architect and landscape designer Charles A Platt. Materials were
chosen for their ageless quality – neutral color aggregate stucco,
salvaged clay tile roof, and reclaimed cypress.
Curtis & Windham Architects

Contributors

ELLIE CULLMAN · CULLMAN & KRAVIS INC. · NEW YORK, NEW YORK

Ellie Cullman is a founding partner of Cullman & Kravis Inc., the distinguished decorating firm in New York City, which she founded with her late partner Hedi Kravis over 30 years ago. Ellie's career has been distinguished by a number of equally impressive achievements. Since 2000, she has been listed in the definitive *Architectural Digest's* AD 100 designated best designers and architects. Additionally, she was included on the AD list of The Deans of American Design in January 2005, and was the recipient of the Stars of Design Award at New York's D&D Building in October 2009. A strong proponent of the arts, Ellie has served as a guest curator at The Museum of American Folk Art. In addition, she is currently a member of the Museum of Modern Art's Contemporary Council and the Metropolitan Museum's Visiting Committee on Objects and Conservation.

KEN TATE · KEN TATE ARCHITECT · NEW ORLEANS, LOUISIANA

Ken Tate received his formal schooling at the Georgia Institute of Technology, the Atlanta School of Art, and Auburn University in Alabama. In 1984, he started his own eponymous firm, and has since designed over 50 homes - proving that traditional architecture not only has a voice, but that it has one with beauty and purpose. Ken is also an accomplished artist, whose non-figurative work has been exhibited throughout the Country and can be found in private collections in New Orleans, New York, Los Angeles, Nashville and Houston.

STEVEN GAMBREL · S.R. GAMBREL, INC. · NEW YORK, NEW YORK

Steven Gambrel is the founder and president of S.R. Gambrel, Inc., an influential interior design firm specializing in both residential and commercial commissions, as well as custom product and furnishings. Having founded his company in 1996, only three years after earning a degree in architecture from the University of Virginia, Steven has been recognized for his endless dedication to creating highly customized interiors and architectural details for each project, as well as his passion for timeless comfortable homes that improve with age. His work is featured consistently in the world's leading publications, and was recently honored as one of "today's greatest talents in architecture and design," in *Architectural Digest's* AD 100.

JOEL BARKLEY · IKE KLIGERMAN BARKLEY ARCHITECTS · NEW YORK, NEW YORK

Joel Barkley is partner at the award winning Ike Kligerman Barkley, the New York and San Francisco based architecture and design firm. An architect as well as a watercolorist, Joel brings a painterly approach to the composition of houses and gardens – where he has illustrated several garden books, and maintains his own organic garden. He received his Master in Architecture from Princeton University, and also attended the Ecoles d'Art Americaines en France Fontainbleau. Together with partners John Ike and Tom Kligerman, Joel has been named as one Architectural Digests leading designers every year since 1995.

DONALD KAUFMAN · DONALD KAUFMAN COLOR · NEW YORK, NEW YORK

Donald Kaufman is one of today's foremost architectural color consultants. He and his wife and design partner, Taffy Dahl, have been creating architectural paint color for more than 30 years. As a pioneer in the field of architectural color, Donald creates pigment formulations based on each color's unique character and performance. Colors are designed with exclusive ingredients, making significant difference in their ability to bring balance and harmony to a room. Donald has developed color schemes for numerous private residences, major museums, art galleries, and public spaces. Recent projects include The American Wing of The Metropolitan Museum in New York and The Kennedy Center Concert Hall in Washington DC.

JOHN ROGERS · PALM BEACH, FLORIDA

John Rogers has a reputation for quality, innovation and customer satisfaction as a result of his experience in building high-end, custom homes for clients from Palm Beach to Miami. Working in a variety of architectural styles, his reputation has been built by assembling a talented team and developing a collaborative atmosphere for the client and their design team. John's experience in the luxury home building market combined with his background in business and finance has enabled him to relate well with clients and has added a beneficial perspective to the way luxury custom homes are built. He has collaborated with some the America's finest architects, interior designers, landscape designers and craftspeople.

JAMES DOYLE & KATHRYN HERMAN · DOYLE HERMAN DESIGN ASSOCIATES · GREENWICH, CONNECTICUT

Founded by James Doyle in 1993, and later joined by Kathyrn Herman in 2000, Doyle Herman Design Associates is an award-winning landscape design firm that creates extraordinary design by integrating artistic expression within the contextual perspective of the presented architecture. Prior to 1993, James was head of a Russell Page garden in his native Ireland. Together with this horticultural experience and a strong design philosophy, James and Kathryn are able create unique and innovative landscapes. The firm's designs have garnered several awards, including the 2010 APLD International Designer of the Year.

KAHLIL HAMADY · HAMADY ARCHITECTS · BOSTON, MASSACHUSETTS

A native of Lebanon, Kahlil Hamady received his primary education at the French school of the "Lycee Franco Libanais" in Beirut. Following a two year apprenticeship with Copper Robertson in New York City, he continued his practice with the internationally renowned landscape designer Francois Goffinet, working on high end residential and landscape projects throughout the United States and Europe. While residing in England, he served as the principal architect for the landscape works at Glympton Park, a 10,000 acre estate in Oxfordshire. In 1997 he founded Hamady Architects, expanding the practice of collaborative artistic and crafted works to the three interrelated subjects of Architecture, Landscape and Interior designs.

FRANCIS TERRY · QUINLAN & FRANCIS TERRY ARCHITECTS · ESSEX, ENGLAND

Since qualifying as an architect in 1994 from Cambridge University, Francis Terry has worked with his father Quinlan Terry. Together they operate one of the most celebrated and influential architectural firms practicing today. Francis is a gifted artist, and regularly exhibits drawings at the *Royal Academy*, and won the Worshipful Company of Architects Prize for Architectural Drawing in 2002. For his artistic paintings he has won the Silver Medal for Portraiture from the Royal Society of Portrait Painters and the Windsor and Newton Young Artist Award.

FOSTER REEVE · FOSTER REEVE & ASSOCIATES · NEW YORK & LOS ANGELES

Foster Reeve, President of Foster Reeve & Associates, holds an MFA from Parsons School of Design. His passion for design led him in 1992 to found his own company, to singularly pursue the craft of traditional plasterwork. Foster's mission is to ignite interest in plaster in the design community and promote its use as the best material choice for quality trim and decoration. He specializes in custom-designed plaster moldings, ornamentation and bas relief, as well as integral color stuc pierre, scagliola, and a host of decorative wall finishes. His work adorns major projects around the world.

CARL SORENSON · THE NANZ COMPANY · NEW YORK, NEW YORK

Carl Sorenson co-founded The Nanz Company in 1989 with Steve Nanz. They started their business by refurbishing existing hardware for pre-war apartment renovations. At the behest of their clients they began making replacement hardware for renovations, which in turn prompted them to develop their own line of hardware. Today, The Nanz Company offers over 3,000 distinct products in a vast array of finishes, all manufactured in the company's 50,000-square-foot (4,645-square-meter) Long Island factory. Nanz operates showrooms in New York, Miami, Houston, Greenwich, Chicago, Los Angeles, and London.

The façade of this new Chicago townhouse includes cut Indiana limestone, buff Norman brick, and a Greene County Corolina granite base, and is designed to look as if it has been there since the turn of the last century.
Liederbach & Graham Architects

The Villa Ravello in Montecito follows in California's long tradition of Spanish Mediterranean style homes.
Appleton & Associates

CARL LAUBIN · HERTFORDSHIRE, ENGLAND

A native of New York, Carl Laubin studied architecture at Cornell University before moving to England in 1973, where he worked for a succession of architects. Carl credits architect Jeremy Dixon for launching his new career as a painter, when he was commissioned to paint depictions of the 1987 redevelopment of the Royal Opera House. Since then, he has produced paintings for a variety of leading classical architects, most notably Leon Krier and John Simpson. Most recently Carl has received wide acclaim for his *capricci* celebrating the work of individual architects such as Palladio, Wren, Hawksmoor, Vanbrugh, Cockerell, Krier, Outram, Ledoux, and Lutyens.

BEN PENTREATH · BEN PENTREATH LTD. · LONDON, ENGLAND

Ben Pentreath opened his architectural practice in 2004. A decade later, the firm is still small in size but works to many different scales, from large-scale urban and master-planning projects to the design of one-off houses, interior decoration, and furniture. In 2008, Ben opened a tiny eponymous design store, which has become one of the most influential small shops in London. Ben's aesthetic is inspired by tradition and a respect for carefully detailed authentic materials and design, but combined with a love of contemporary culture, which means that life is never dull. He writes regularly for the *Financial Times*.

JOHN MILNER · JOHN MILNER ARCHITECTS · CHADDS FORD, PENNSYLVANIA

John Milner is a respected and widely published architect with a career-long passion for historic preservation and new traditional design. His particular expertise is in the detailed analysis of historic buildings to document their physical and cultural history, and the development of strategies and technical procedures for their restoration, conservation and adaptive use. Prior to starting his architectural practice in 1968, John was employed as a staff architect for the Historic American Building Survey and Branch of Restorations of the U.S. National Park Service. He has taught at the University of Pennsylvania's Graduate School of design for over thirty years, receiving the *Perkins Award for Distinguished Teaching* in 2007.

LYNNE SCALO · LYNNE SCALO DESIGN · GREENWICH, CONNECTICUT

Lynne Scalo has more than a decade of interior design experience. Her sophisticated yet functional design aesthetic reflects her ability to seamlessly blend modern glamour with classic elegance, transcending both staid traditionalism and faddish trends, instilling timelessness to all her projects. Lynne has designed projects with clients in Connecticut, Manhattan, the Hamptons, Nantucket, Palm Beach, Aspen, London, and Frankfurt. A keen observer of life's nuances, Lynne's design is widely respected for the art and integrity shown in its approach to every project. A world traveler with an eye for fashion and an extensive background in fine arts, Lynne also works with her clients on developing and expanding their art collections.

BARBARA SALLICK · WATERWORKS · DANBURY, CONNECTICUT

Barbara Sallick co-founded Waterworks in 1978 with her husband, Robert, and serves as the company's senior vice president of design. She is the arbiter of Waterworks influential design aesthetic and oversees creative decisions that span from the details of product development to the logistics of store layouts. Using her education and lifelong interest in art and travel, Barbara employs formal principles of architecture and decoration to elevate the bath to a space that is as beautiful, personal and inviting as it is practical. Waterworks now operates multiple showrooms nationally and internationally, including new locations in London and New York.

WILLIAM BATES III · THE AMERICAN COLLEGE OF THE BUILDING ARTS · CHARLESTON, SOUTH CAROLINA

William Bates founded the Drawing and Design Department at the American College of the Building Arts in 2005, where he continues as a full professor lecturing on classical drawing principles and aesthetics. He is a Fellow of the Institute of Classical Architecture and Art, where he founded and supports the Edward Vason Jones Rome Scholarship, in memory of his late mentor. As an accomplished designer in his own right, William also specializes in American Furniture and Decorative Arts (1800–1840), with a focus on construction methods and conservation. His formal education includes a Bachelor of Interior Design from Auburn University and a Master of Architecture from the University of Miami.

Photography & Drawing Credits

PHOTOGRAPHY :

JEAN ALLSOPP: 140, 141, 142, 143, 144, 145

JAN BALDWIN: 106

PAUL BARKER: 222, 223, 224, 225

SIMON BEVAN: 102, 107

JUNE BUCK: 79, 80

NICK CARTER: 2-3, 209, 226, 227, 228, 229

TOM CRANE: 113, 184, 185, 187, 188, 189, 239

JOHN CRITCHLEY: 206, 207, 255

SHEPPARD DAY: 21

ERICA GEORGE DINES: 152, 153

TIMOTHY DUNFORD: 14-15, 28, 32, 61, 216, 217, 218, 219, 220, 221, 240

EMILY JENKINS FOLLOWILL: 17, 154, 155

JAMES GARRISON: 186

GEOFFREY GROSS: 111, 112

DAVID HAMSLEY: 54

PAUL HIGHNAM: 132, 133, 134, 136

NICK JOHNSON: 8, 12-13

RICHARD JOHNSON: 130, 156, 157, 158, 159

ERIK KVALSIVIK: 236, 237, 238

NEIL LANDINO JNR: 5, 64, 67, 68

DAVID DUNCAN LIVINGSTON: 26

PETER MARGONELLI: 50

MATTHEW MILLMAN: 25, 202, 203, 204, 205

DANIEL NEWCOMB: 86

PETER OLSON: 243

DON PEARSE: 108

ERIC PIASECKI: Front Cover, 11, 23, 44, 47, 48, 49, 176, 177, 178, 179

TIM STREET PORTER: 114, 117, 118, 119

AUSTEN REDMAN (FRANCIS JOHNSON & PARTNERS): 174, 175, 176, 177

JASON ROSENBERG: 53

KIM SARGENT (SARGENT ARCHITECTURAL PHOTOGRAPHY): 58, 62, 210, 211, 212, 213, 214, 215

DURSTON SAYLOR: 27, 38, 41, 42, 43, 168, 169, 170, 171, 172, 173, 190, 191, 192, 193, 194, 195

TONY SOLURI: 178, 179, 251

GREG TINIUS: 255

ALEX VERTIKOFF: 136, 137, 138, 139

MATTHEW WALLA: 252

JONATHAN WALLEN: Inside Sleeve, 18, 22, 24, 196, 197, 198, 199, 200, 201, 230, 231, 232, 233, 234, 235, 242, 246

WADE ZIMMERMAN: 1, 160, 161, 162, 163

DRAWINGS & RENDERINGS:

STEPHEN DAVIS: 16, 63, 245

CARL LAUBIN: 20, 94, 98-99, 101

REDFISH RENDERING LLC: 36-37

HAMADY ARCHITECTS LLC: 166

GEORGE SAUMAREZ SMITH: 208

FRANCIS TERRY: 29

LESLIE–JON VICKORY: 256

COURTESY OF:

THE AMERICAN COLLEGE OF THE BUILDING ARTS: 126

CURTIS & WINDHAM ARCHITECTS: 6, 146, 147, 148, 149, 150, 151, 248
(These photographs are from the forthcoming book tentatively titled *A Monograph on the Work of Curtis & Windham Architects* and used by permission of Curtis & Windham Architects Inc, and Texas A&M University Press)

HAMADY ARCHITECTS LLC: 71, 72, 75, 164, 165, 167

DONALD KAUFMAN COLOR: 56, 57

THE NANZ COMPANY: 19 top, 88, 91, 92, 93

BEN PENTREATH: 105

FOSTER REEVE & ASSOCIATES: 19 bottom, 30, 82, 85, 87

QUINLAN & FRANCIS TERRY ARCHITECTS: 76

WATERWORKS: 120, 123, 124, 125

The plan for this new house in Hampshire explores the heritage of Palladianism developed in England in the eighteenth century, and is based upon Palladio's un-built plan for the Villa Ragona at Le Ghizzole.
George Saumarez Smith, ADAM Architecture